Psalms of the Heart

Psalms of the Heart

by

JOHN MACBEATH, M.A., D.D.

~

*To every lover
of the Psalms*

~

AMBASSADOR

Psalms of the Heart
© Copyright Ambassador Productions Ltd.

ISBN   1   898787   27   1

Printed and Published by
AMBASSADOR PRODUCTIONS LTD
Providence House
16 Hillview Avenue,
Belfast, BT5 6JR

CONTENTS

Contents

7

Contents

Contents

FOREWORD

THOSE who desire a critical study of the Psalms have an ample literature; those also who seek a detailed exposition of the Book have a library at their service; many writers have discussed the historical context of the Psalms, devotional works and volumes of annotations are also ready to hand. The present book is simply an attempt to put in brief and direct form some significant and useful lesson plucked out of the heart of each psalm.

In the Psalms all differences of race and space and time are transcended; here is the universal language of all moods of the human spirit, and of all the ages of man's life on the earth. "The Psalms attract the young, invigorate the active, enliven the contemplative, and encircle with a peaceful glory the venerable brow of age."

"In the Bible," said Luther, "we look into the heart of all the saints"; this is pre-eminently true of the Psalms, which make a little Bible of their own. Here we look into the heart of sinners as well as saints, and are made deeply aware that "They who fain would serve Thee best, are conscious most of wrong within". Contrition and comfort have their perfect expression; encouragement too for them that stumble by the way. "He that would be wise, let him read the Proverbs; he that would be holy, let him read the Psalms"; they will cheer him in his high endeavour.

Peter Mathieson was Sir Walter Scott's coachman. To him religion was something taught, for it meant instruction, and it was something caught because it was infectious as music. Sir Walter's "evening stroll" took him to the bowling green beside the coachman's cottage, but, "In truth, I wished to have a smooth walk and a canny seat for myself within earshot of Peter's evening psalm."

"When I find I cannot make headway in devotion," wrote James Gilmour, "I open the Bible at the Psalms and push in my canoe, and let myself be carried along in the stream of devotion which flows through the whole book; the current always sets towards God and in most places is strong and deep."

Regarding history, dates, authorship, editorial selections, divisions of the whole book and other matters, an exhaustive literature is available, and I am not unfamiliar with it. But there are many who will appreciate the refreshing freedom and undoubted value of Dr. John A. Hutton's statement of mind: "For myself I like to think that the Psalms for the most part were written in secret, and that those who wrote them desired to remain unknown. I am thankful, too, that we are not very sure of the date at which any particular psalm was written. For the truth is, in the case of each, the writer is 'Everyman'. As for dates, the setting of each psalm is—any stage in human history when the soul of man has been so startled or so relieved that it has become tender enough to adopt the language of a psalm as its own."

This book is for the wayfarer who has not the time nor the opportunity for expository or exegetical studies, but must put his book in his wallet and sally forth to his daily avocation, a wayfarer among men, a lover of his country, his church, and his God.

"Enough—

That all the jarring notes of life
    Seem blending in a psalm,
And all the angles of its strife,
    Slow rounding into calm.

And so the shadows fall apart,
    And so the west winds play;
And all the windows of my heart
    I open to the day."

J. M.

BOOK I

PSALMS I–41

From ancient times the Psalms have been divided into five books. Each book ends with a doxology; the 150th Psalm being itself the doxology of the fifth book and of the whole collection. The attempt has also been made to establish correspondence between the five books of the Psalter and the five books of the Pentateuch.

Of the occasion of every Psalm there is often no trace left in history. From the first of the Psalms it is clear that the Hebrew lived close to Nature which to him was the workshop of God. His parables are drawn from the growing things of pasture and woodland, sheep and cattle, mountain and desert, field and forest; all of them in succession are used to express the reactions of the human spirit to the vicissitudes of life.

If you take the Psalms for company you take a sure guide and a wise interpreter for company. You will not travel far before you know the Lord for your Shepherd; or you may experience slips and stumbles and falls, and your deliverance may repeat the story of the lift of God; "He took me from a fearful pit and from the miry clay and set my feet upon a rock, and established my goings; He put a new song in my mouth." This is the typical experience of religion. From the guilty sobbing of our sinfulness He lifts us to the singing levels of His redemption.

THE DIFFERENCE BETWEEN

"Blessed is the man . . ."

THE book opens with a beatitude pronounced upon the man to whom religion is a gladsome thing; it is an inseparable part of his essential life.

The difference between one sort of man and another, the fundamental difference is not a social distinction as between rich and poor; nor an emotional difference as between the happy and unhappy; nor a racial difference as between white and coloured people, nor a difference of dialect or language. The essential difference is between those who believe and those who do not believe in God. The psalm deals with two different types of men. Our Lord identified Himself with this distinction: "He that is not with me is against me"; and again, "He that is not against us is for our part." That is our Lord's grouping of the people of His time and ours.

The difference between the two types of men reveals itself in a variety of ways. The difference is recognisable in the company they keep. "Birds of a feather flock together." They have some common interest, some bond of intimate concern, whether good or bad, whether scornful of religion or sincerely devoted to it. The difference reveals itself in the books they read; every man has his own library according to his taste and preference. The distinction here is very pronounced. For one man, it is the counsel of the ungodly, the way of sinners, the seats of scoffers. For the other man, his delight is in the law of the Lord; his ardent soul meditates on it day and night; it is the subject of ceaseless interest, the unending quest of truth and ever more truth. Bunyan's pilgrim started out in his quest with a book in his hand. The Book made him a pilgrim, and it kept him company to the end. Bunyan's Bible was his daily bread.

The difference reveals itself in the habits they cultivate, and in the final results. The difference is permanent and works out to a destiny. The one type is like a tree planted by rivers of water and bearing fruit in its season; the other type is like chaff driven before the wind. Those who order their lives by the law of God have touched the permanence of things; not theirs the sorrowful confession, "My way of life is fallen into the sere and yellow leaf." Their leaf is ever green, they have something in them that is proof against decay, the fundamental sources of the universe give them perpetual life. These two types, the flimsy chaff and the evergreen tree, are opposites to the poet's mind. No man can have it both ways.

THE MESSIANIC PURPOSE

" The uttermost possession."

"Ask of Me, and I will give thee the uttermost parts of the
earth for thy possession." God's passion, God's power, and God's
purpose are on the scale of the uttermost.

Revolt is the first accent of the Psalm: not primarily the revolt
of Israel, but the revolt of those outside the Covenant, the
Gentile peoples. They formed an alliance against Jehovah and
against His people, to break up their institutions. In the fulness
of time Christ overcomes the distinctions that provoke hatred.
He claims universal relationship with the race; all others are
limited by nationality: Moses was Hebrew, Confucius was
Chinese, Buddha was Indian, Socrates was Greek, Mohammed
was Arab, but no one can say with the same meaning that Jesus
was Hebrew; He was the Son of Man, relating Himself without
distinction of race or tongue to all mankind, down to the last
and the least of the human family.

Retribution follows upon revolt. The contest is hopelessly un-
equal. Who can take arms against the Almighty and prosper?
At first Jehovah holds His hand, and then He takes action in
judgment. He will not always chide, neither will He always keep
silence. Resistance to Him will at last be shattered like a potter's
vessel. Racial prejudices have established distinctions that have
produced bitterness, persecution and war; but these angers and
strifes are not for ever. Christ will make a full end of all mischief,
and at the last none will dispute His rule. Hence the strategy
of this ancient counsel of wisdom and discretion to all rulers,
judges, peoples.

Reconciliation is the final act of the Psalm. "Kiss the Son. . . .
Blessed are all they that put their trust in Him": Christ is the
great Reconciler of men to God, and of men to one another in all
the relationships of nations and peoples. "He is able to save to
the uttermost all who come unto God by Him." He intends that
the Kingdom of God shall embrace all peoples, reconcile all
classes, and make one redeemed society. That purpose embraces
the community where you live, the street that holds your house.
The eyes of a fool are in the ends of the earth, but the eyes of a
wise man are in his head; he sees his opportunity from his own
doorstep.

Your doorstep is the uttermost part of the earth to those who
live at the other end of the world. Give God's purpose a start
where you are; your effort may secure a new foothold for His
Kingdom.

A SONG OF THE MORNING

" I awaked, for the Lord sustained me."

THE song was born in a troubled heart. The singer had been in sore straits; amongst other things his foes reproached him with the fact that even God did nothing for him. It is said that the song of a bird in a cage is not always a song of gladness, sometimes it is a cry of pain, a protest against imprisonment. This is the wistful song of a caged life.

The concern that disturbed him: "Lord, how are they increased that trouble me." Their number is impressive, "ten thousands of people have set themselves against me"; their defiance was strong, for they said "there is no help for him in God". His religion afforded him no advantage, so it seemed to the blind man, but there is always more in life than meets the eye, especially the eye that does not wish to see all there is to see.

The courage that sustained him is cheerfully confessed, "Thou, O Lord, art a shield for me, I will not be afraid." His enemies were like wild beasts, eager to devour, but God would take away their power to hurt him. He recalls God's help in the past and he is confident of its continuance.

> Art thou afraid His strength shall fail
>   When comes the evil day?—
> And can an all-creating arm
>   Grow weary or decay?

The confidence that composed him. Although threatened by mischief he was not afraid to go to sleep at night: "I laid me down and slept, I awakened for the Lord sustained me." The divine presence was his protection against outward hostility and inward dispeace. He hid himself in God and said farewell to fear. In this security he slept and awakened with a song.

> Still, still with Thee, when purple morning breaketh,
>   When the bird waketh, and the shadows flee:
> Fairer than morning, lovelier than the daylight,
>   Dawns the sweet consciousness, I am with Thee.

A SONG OF THE EVENING

"Commune with your own heart upon your bed."

THE most durable metal in ancient arts was Corinthian bronze, produced by the fusion of various metals when Corinth was burned. Adversity ceases to be adversity when it is followed by some gain that could not otherwise be found.

The productiveness of trouble is celebrated, "Thou hast enlarged me when I was in distress." The singer has found advantage in his affliction, he has gathered recompense from trial. It is probable that we would not have had *Paradise Lost* if Milton had not been blind. We might not have had Beethoven's music if Beethoven had not been deaf. Wisdom was shut out at one entrance, but these men found light elsewhere. If their powers were limited at one point they were liberated at another.

The profit of self-communion is implied in the saying that if and when other sources fail: Try nearer home, try the sources within: "Commune with your own heart in silence." Thomas à Kempis advises all who desire true contrition to build a secret chamber, to enter it and shut out the tumults of the world in expectation that the thoughts of the secret place would prove a precious possession. Somewhere, somehow, you must leave the noisy world outside, you must shut the door against its intrusion, saying, with Charles Kingsley: "Leave me alone, let me think."

The provision that prayer brings of peace and felicity is the concluding testimony: "For Thou, Lord, only makest me to dwell in safety." The comforts of prayer are an unfailing support, and no human power can prevent its exercise. Listen to a prisoner in the Tower of London: "Oh, you ministers of evil, whoever you be, visible or invisible, you shall not build a wall between my God and me. I have something within me that grows stronger and stronger as times grow more and more evil."

> O Lord, Who by Thy presence hast made light
> The heat and burden of the toilsome day,
> Be with me also in the silent night,
> Be with me when the daylight fades away.

THE TERMS OF DEVOTION

" I will come into Thy house."

THE soul's approach to God has six different expressions: "Give ear to my words." Words articulate the thoughts of the mind and the emotions of the heart. They may not always completely express our feelings, but they are necessary to help another to understand what we want and what we mean. "Take with you words, and turn to the Lord: speak unto Him" (Hosea 14. 2).

"Consider my meditation." This is the deeper exercise, words are empty unless they carry the mind with them: "My words fly up, my thoughts remain below, words without thoughts never to heaven go." But thoughts without words may travel to the Throne.

"Hearken to my cry" adds another term. A cry is a short, sharp, urgent appeal; its thought is swift, its words are few. An infant has no language but a cry, but it is enough for a mother, and for God.

And what am I?
An infant crying in the night;
An infant crying for the light,
And with no language but a cry.

"Prayer", petition is included. "In the morning will I direct my prayer unto Thee." It means something deliberate, the studied expression of worship; it is the regular habit and frequent exercise of the spirit.

O Thou by Whom we come to God.
The Life, the Truth, the Way;
The path of prayer Thyself hast trod.
Lord, teach us how to pray.

"My voice shalt Thou hear." There are silences that are unbearable, as when the lonely heart aches for the sound of a voice that is still. Has God any ground of complaint because of your silence to Him? He gave us power of speech but we are often dumb creatures to Himself.

"I will look up." There is devotion in a look; the petition of the eyes may be more wistful and persuasive than the petition of the lips. A look may say more than language. A look is never so inviting as when it summons God: "Prayer is the upward glancing of an eye when none but God is near." The lifted eye draws the attention of God. "There is life for a look"—never was so much dependent upon so little (Num. 21. 9).

18

A THREEFOLD PLEA

" The Lord will receive my prayer."

OUR prayers are rarely simple enough for us to say "One thing have I desired of the Lord." We commonly ask for many things and often the wrong thing. It is not the patient's right to prescribe for the physician; that is the physician's prerogative. "I used to ask for many things—now I only ask for God." God is the Physician to Whom the psalmist submits the symptoms of his trouble and ventures his requests.

The first petition confesses weakness and distress, and seeks the compassion of God. "Have mercy upon me, O Lord, for I am weak: O Lord heal me. My bones are vexed, my soul is also vexed." The Psalmist is in bad condition. Adversities, difficulties, disabilities have overtaken him as they overtake most of us. These experiences are not always the consequence of guilt; they are part of the discipline sent to prove, correct and purify God's people. "Endurance is the crowning quality, and patience all the passion of great hearts." He gives power to the faint and to those who have no might to stand up to the stern experiences of life, He supplies strength. There is supreme value in staying power, in the ability to hold on and to hold out when everything depends upon the resolve not to give way or to lose heart.

The second petition confesses weariness, dejection, and asks for courage. "O save me for Thy mercies sake . . . I am weary with my groaning." We grow tired of most things, tired of work and of idleness, tired of company and of ourselves, tired of believing —we want to see; tired of hoping—we want to have the thing hoped for! The compassion of heaven alone can give us patience and sustain our confidence. If, as Samuel Butler put it, "Life is one long process of getting tired," it may also be one long experience of the refreshments of God.

The third petition makes sorrow a plea for comfort. "All the night I make my bed to swim, I water my couch with tears— the Lord hath heard the voice of my weeping." Sensitiveness melts the strong. It is a great thing to be able to remain sensitive; it is easy to lose it, then we become hard and indifferent. There is safety in sensitiveness—Peter went out and wept bitterly! The tears of repentance gained the swift comforts of Christ. He heals the wounded spirit. "Comfort ye, comfort ye, My people," is God's commission to His servants; His comfort is of the strong and heartening quality that puts men on their feet. There is a sympathy that makes men soft, a comfort that weakens them; the comfort of God makes men and women strong, resolute, competent.

"WITHOUT CAUSE"

" Mine enemy without cause."

IT has been said that it is our dislikes that make life interesting! They always give us something to talk about; we talk ourselves into a sense of virtue by talking down other people.

The plea we make against any dislike of ourselves is that we have done nothing to provoke dislike. That is the argument of the writer of the psalm; other people are his enemies "without cause". He was innocent of any occasion of offence, he was unaware of having done any wrong that would arouse against him the prejudice of other people.

The plea was made for Christ by prophet and apostle, "They hated Me without a cause." If they found occasion of offence against Him, it was not because of any hurt or wrong that He had done, it was because the good that He had done was unwelcome and the truths that He had taught were unacceptable. When a crowd of angry Jews threatened to stone Him, Jesus urged, "Many good works have I showed you from my Father; for which of those works do you stone Me?" Prejudice and ignorance mounted against Him. In the day of His trial, Pilate declared, "I find no fault in Him," but the intolerant crowd shouted for His execution. "They hated me without a cause" are among the saddest reflections in Scripture. He revealed the sins of the world and men revolted from their own uncovered wrong.

The plea was made by the apostle Paul that believers should be "blameless and harmless, the children of God without rebuke in the midst of a crooked and perverse nation". But they shared the reproach of Christ as He had forewarned them: "If they have persecuted Me they will also persecute you." The bitterest enemy of the followers of Christ was Saul of Tarsus. He vowed to wipe out the infant Church, but Christ captured and changed him, and he became the foremost apostle. The tables were turned on him; the persecutor had changed sides and became himself the target of spite and the victim of persecution. "I persecuted the Church of Christ; I did it in ignorance," he confessed with deep sorrow. The sins of ignorance are one of the sorrows of God. The prayer is ever relevant, "Father, forgive them, for they know not what they do." To be disliked for Christ's sake is very different from being disliked because some fault or flaw in ourselves spoils every good thing in us. Make it your business to remove every just cause of offence, take away every occasion of stumbling, aspire to be "without blame". Let the good in you be so good that you cannot easily be falsely accused.

THE MINDFULNESS OF GOD

" Thou art mindful."

THE mindfulness of God is deliberate. It is not an incidental remembrance. It is an essential act.

It is selective. It is only part of the duty of the memory to hold things in remembrance; the other part is to forget things. All things are not worthy of being kept in mind; there is much that is better forgotten. "I will not remember thy sins," is a welcome word. God is mindful of us, but our forgiven sins are forgotten sins. Here is the pattern of a disciplined memory, a memory that chooses what is to be remembered and what is to be dismissed from recollection.

It is recollective. His mindfulness is habitual, it is not merely occasional, a thought of us now and then, when it occurs to Him; it is more constant than a mother's; "She may forget, yet will I not forget thee." It is inclusive, His habitual recollection embraces all our needs. He gives personal attention to our wants, visits us Himself with mercies, proving again and again that not the least little thing essential to our good is ever neglected or overlooked.

It is productive. The mindfulness of God is not merely a mental attitude, an act of thought and nothing more. It is executive; it does things in heaven and in earth, among angels and men; it fixes our rank, our place, our duty. Constantly we stand within the active thought and purpose of God; He associates us with himself in the redemption of the world and the furthering of His purpose for mankind. When I was posted temporarily to an Australian unit during the war, I arrived at their camp after midnight and had my first service at 7 a.m. At the close of the service a number of the men gathered round me to inform me that I was unanimously "counted in". By this formula I was accounted a comrade, I was accorded a place in their trust and affection, my life was identified with theirs in one endeavour after victory. Sir Wilfred Grenfell, of Labrador fame, has told us that at the outset of his life his one desire was not so much to be saved; he wanted to be used, his passion was to be "counted in", to be identified with something God wanted to be done in his generation and by him. To be wanted by God is distinction enough. That is why you are here. He is counting on you.

KNOWLEDGE AND TRUST

"They that know will trust."

THERE is a sense in which trust is dependent upon knowledge, "They that know Thy name will put their trust in Thee." A great English essayist said that he never hated any man he knew. Knowledge disabused the mind of suspicion and dislike. Suspicion departed upon acquaintance. Some people grow on you, intimacy encourages trust. The more you know them, the more you trust them.

But there is also a sense in which knowledge is dependent upon trust. You must begin by believing in other people. Give them the benefit of your confidence, help them with the assurance that you are relying upon them as to life and character and everything else. We have a saying that you should trust all men until you find them out! Give them the support of your belief. Raise the level of your reasoning to the experiment of action: "If any man will do—he shall know" (John vii. 17). A lady of rank and title was long anxious to reach some certitude of faith. So tense was her spirit one evening that she left her guests happily engaged, and walked in her garden; in the new stillness, as if someone had waited for her coming, a mystic voice whispered: "Act as if I was, and you will find I am." She put it to the proof and it worked. Abraham believed God, and he went out not knowing whither he went! Columbus did not wait for knowledge of America; he trusted first and found knowledge next.

There is a further sense in which the two hang together. The poet suggests an antithesis: "We have but faith, we cannot know; for knowledge is of things we see. And yet we trust it comes from Thee, a beam in darkness, let it grow." Trust persists, "Oh yet we trust that somehow good will be the final goal of ill"; and yet the crave for knowledge is persistent too, "Behold we know not anything, we can but trust that good shall fall, at last—far off—at last, to all, and every winter change to spring." Trust and knowledge are not opposites; they are complementary. Jesus was hindered in His activities by the unbelief of the people. If they had trusted Him they would have known Him, but their distrust deprived them of so great a possession. Unbelief stands outside in the dark and knows nothing; faith enters a room of light and knows all.

> O make but trial of His love;
> Experience will decide,
> How blest are they, and only they
> Who in His truth confide.

ALTITUDES

" Far above out of sight."

THAT "God sits in His heaven and does nothing" is the complaint of those who protest against the apparent absence of God from His universe: "Why standest Thou afar off, O Lord! Why hidest Thou Thyself in time of trouble?" The same argument encourages the covetous, crafty, unscrupulous man in his selfish pursuits: "He says in his heart, God hides His face—He will never see it." The writer reassures himself that God sees all.

Thrice blest is he to whom is given the instinct that can tell
That God is on the field when He is most invisible.

Some things are beyond our grasp, "Thy judgments are far above." Things within the range of our grasp are modestly near, "but a man's reach should exceed his grasp, or what's a heaven for?" Some things are within our grasp, let us not despise them because they are near. All life is not mystery, there are some great certitudes we can hold with both hands, but happily for us there are some things too big for us to hold. They exceed the measure of our grasp.

Some things are beyond our reach. Bunyan confessed that the women of Bedford, talking together in the sun, were speaking of things far above, out of his reach. They discoursed of the new birth and of other things unfamiliar to him, and were as if they had found a new world. Some people have a great reach, they eclipse the rest of us in the traffic they have with the world above.

Ah! God is other than we think; His ways are far above,
Far beyond reason's height, and reached Only by childlike love.

Some things are beyond our sight: "Thy judgments are far above, out of his sight." When one thing is incomparably better than another thing, we say it is "out of sight" better. The difference is incalculable. It is so with the gifts of God. "Eye hath not seen the things God hath prepared for them that love Him." They eclipse the best things men have ever looked on, therefore you can anticipate the future, be it near or be it far, not merely with serene assurance, but with eager expectancy.

AS A BIRD TO ITS MOUNTAIN

" Flee as a bird."

THERE is a wealth of suggestion in the aviary of Scripture. Its bird life yields an attractive imagery. In literature and in legend the bird is an image of the soul. The flutter of wings is familiar; wings of a dove, wings of an eagle are here; sparrow and swallow appear. Birds are expressive symbols of human moods: "I am like a pelican of the wilderness; I am like an owl of the desert; I am as a sparrow alone upon the house top" (Ps. 102). "How say you to my soul, Flee as a bird to your mountain?"

The counsel we give to others is commonly based upon some experience of our own. David hid himself in the mountains from the pursuit of Saul. There God covered him with His cloak and kept him from harm. There is always in the human heart the conviction that some happy experience can be repeated. God does not exhaust His power by one deliverance, rather does He create the expectation that, if need be, He will do it again; "As the mountains are round about Jerusalem so the Lord is round about His people."—"Flee as a bird to the mountains."

The choice of retreat is fundamental to the Hebrew mind. The mountains were the habitation of God, the stepping-stones of Deity. Their summits directed the gaze of the watchful to the heavens from whence come all true help. Much of the history of the Hebrew race is associated with the mountains. On the up-lands of the earth the Hebrew heart felt itself near to God's seat. In the fastnesses of the hills they built their shrines; they erected their altars where the eagle builds its nest.

The custody of God is available for all who seek it. Not merely is the seclusion of the hills a means of safety—"my help cometh from the Lord who made heaven and earth". Personal trust seeks a personal response, mind answering to mind and heart to heart. There is no effectual escape except that which God Himself provides; He alone is the fugitive's safe cover. "The swallow hath found a nest for herself, even thine altars" (Ps. 84). Here is nesting in peace under God's eaves, safe under the shadow of the Almighty.

> Flight from Him is vainest questing,
> Flight to Him is safest nesting.

ARE GOOD PEOPLE SCARCE?

" The godly man ceaseth."

WHERE does the problem of scarcity touch us most keenly? There might be a serious shortage of money, of bread, of employment, of goodwill; the complaint here is that "the godly man ceaseth".

> Ill fares the land, to hast'ning ills a prey,
> Where wealth accumulates and men decay.

The scarcity of godly people involved for Sodom and Gomorrah a more tragic plight than shortage of food in Europe during the wars. We cannot put one scarcity against another; the shortage of any good thing is a serious deprivation for any people, but we cannot forget that a nation's truest asset is its people, and their value is enormously enhanced when they are good people. Character-values have priority in the judgment of heaven. The godly life has a vicarious importance beyond any economic assessment: "God blessed the house of Pharaoh for Joseph's sake."

The shortage of good people is a nation's worst bankruptcy; "There is none that doeth good; no, not one." This is a simple statement of fact without any attempt at explanation. A difficult environment is never to be accepted as a pretext for, or an explanation of, the absence of godliness: Daniel resisted the evil contagion of Babylon; he kept himself unspotted from its excess. Even in Sardis there were people who kept their garments from defilement, the white life defied the city's wickedness.

The shortage may occur through persecution, through fear, through the departure of the godly to another place, through the suppression of liberty, the crushing of religion. It may be brought about by the apathy and indifference of God's people who have lapsed from their first estate, and are no longer the conscience of the community or the guardians of a people's trust. How fares the land in your corner of it?

HOW LONG? HOW LONG?

"Wilt Thou forget me?"

"IF YOU can direct me to anything more exquisite than the thirteenth psalm," wrote Marcus Dods to his sister Marcia, "I will follow your direction with a happiness not often attaching to earthly pursuits." The psalm starts in shadow and ends in sunlight.

The language of complaint is never long silent in a world like this and in a life like ours. The provocation of it arises from a hundred quarters. When the spirit of complaining takes hold of us it is well to get the complaint out. To speak it brings a certain ease of inward strain. The complaint is made that God has forgotten, that He has withdrawn His interest, that the soul is overcome with sorrow and the enemy exults himself in triumph. Four times the singer asks "How long" these things are to continue. It is an insistent cry: Has God no care?

The cure of the complaint comes when he turns his complaining into a prayer. He refers his distress direct to the Almighty. Each complaint becomes the subject of petition having in view the glory that would be God's if He would deliver His servant, the good influence it would have upon his enemy, the advantage that would be his own. "Come quickly," wrote Lord Mountjoy when urging Erasmus to visit England. "Come quickly. Do not torture us with expectation." It is the plea of the psalmist to a greater than Erasmus, troubled as he was by the delays of God.

Confidence follows at once. Fears give place to trust, and the speech of complaining is turned to the language of a song, "I will sing because He hath dealt bountifully with me." Try this short way with your complaining when next the dark mood strikes you. Telling your troubles to a friend reduces them by half, telling them to God cancels them out. He changes our griefs and grievances so that they no longer rasp our spirit. You bring Him a sorrow, you carry away a song.

> O say not thou art left of God,
>   Because His tokens in the sky
> Thou canst not read; this earth He trod
>   To teach thee He is ever nigh.

RECOVERY OF THE REPROBATE

"There is none that doeth good."

THE reprobate state of a people is the long sorrow of God. It is
not a reprobate heart but a reprobate generation that is under
review. The writer's judgment upon his time is that it is so
corrupt that "no one is doing good". Widespread evil is the
disease of his time; society is so deluged with wrong that there
is neither ark nor righteous man to deliver or be delivered from
its darksome flood. The root of its evil is its practical denial of
God.

The research of God Himself is quoted to verify the condition
of society: "Jehovah looked from heaven upon the sons of men
to see if there were any seeking after God—there is not even one."
The divine heart yearned to find hearts that were turned toward
itself, and the result was sore disappointment. What God wanted
to see was very different from what He did see. There was none
looking in His direction. "To make an order understood," wrote
Lord Charles Beresford, "the men must be looking at the officer
who gives it. Silence and attention are the first necessities for
discipline." But God Himself was not given this measure of
courtesy and devotion.

The recovery of the people is the set purpose of God. The
writer foresaw the interventions of God, he foresaw the power
of God frustrating evil, and he anticipated the deliverance that
was sure to come, "when Jehovah brings back the captivity of
His people". From the captivity of misfortune, sorrow, sin,
prejudice, fear or care, He sets His people free. There is no
captivity He cannot break, nor captive He cannot free. Of all
service His alone is perfect freedom.

> Make me a captive, Lord,
> And then I shall be free;
> Force me to render up my sword,
> And I shall conqueror be.

THE GUEST OF GOD

"Who shall sojourn in Thy tabernacle?"

THE safety of the guest is an assured part of Eastern hospitality. The stranger who sought refuge in the tent in the desert or the home in the city was assured of protection. So far as the household could afford it, the guest was sheltered from all harm. The hospitality of God is not less liberal. He provides protection from every foe.

The sanctity of the guest of God is the poet's chief concern. He recognises that the character of the Host determines the character of the guest, and therefore only the man of upright life can be the guest of God. His behaviour is above reproach, he is blameless in his conduct, he is diligent in duty; no act of his does hurt to his neighbour, his vote is not for sale, no money can purchase his support for a wrong or doubtful cause. "Though they cover the canvas with gold and ask me to paint what my conscience does not approve," said Millet, "I will not do it."

The sincerity of the guest of God is an essential quality. His words must be true and his lips free from slander, from flattery, from every form of insincere speech and every charge of broken promises or forgotten vows. Prayer and praise have an unwelcome sound when they are offered by lips that have been stained with slander, gossip, unwholesome wit, sinister talk. "Let no back-biting or talebearing man sit here," was Augustine's defence of his table. Much more does God want approved character in His guests. He insists upon good relations with other people as well as with Himself. To the heart of malice or uncharitableness, to the estranged and embittered spirit, is this qualification given, "First be reconciled to your brother and then come!" Much is expected from the guests of kings, much more is expected from the guests of God.

THEREFORE

"Therefore my heart is glad."

ON August 15th, 1852, Macaulay records in his diary that he went to church and heard what he described as—"Not a bad sermon on the word 'Therefore'." The Psalms make frequent use of this simple and significant word. It generally comes near the end of an argument, with one's self, or with another. It celebrates an answer found, a solution discovered, a conclusion reached. Here it explains a joyous emotion; "Therefore my heart is glad."

It is the gladness of single-minded devotion; "I have set the Lord always before me, because He is at my right hand, I shall not be moved; therefore my heart is glad." The singer proclaims the complete avowal of himself to God. His love is not distracted by any competitive affection. Let others worship idols if they will; as for this man, he worships at no other shrine, he makes sacrifice on no other altar. Jehovah is his choice; to Him and His people he adheres with all his heart. One loyalty commands all his being, and preserves the unity of his life.

It is the gladness of a fixed purpose. The great choice is made, and with that secured, he enjoys satisfying contentment. With Jehovah as his portion he finds the lines are fallen unto him in pleasant places, he has a goodly heritage. Other people may have lands, possessions, honours, but he has Jehovah, and he is the richest and best endowed of all men because none can deprive him of his inheritance. Therefore he resolves to make the most of it. "I have set Jehovah always before me." He is like a man going to develop his estate, going to explore the sufficiency of God for every circumstance of life.

It is the gladness of supreme expectation. He contemplates the far-off consequence of something after death. His experience of God is such that it holds within itself the witness and prophecy of immortality. Whether he would survive death like Moses, or surmount death like Elijah, did not matter; he had got hold of an experience of God that was too good for death to destroy. These immortal longings claim high warrant, and the warrant is here, "In my Father's house are many mansions; if it were not so I would have told you."

WE SLEEP TO WAKE

" I shall be satisfied when I awake."

THAT is the right order; we do not wake that we may sleep again, we sleep that we may wake; sleep is the servant of wakefulness. "I shall be satisfied when I awake," that is, when all our powers are alert and occupied. "I had awakened to the beauty of the world," said Sir Martin Conway of his early exhilaration of the summits of the hills.

There is an awakening of pain. One bravely asked that if through some lassitude he had failed—"Lord, Thy most pointed pleasure take and stab my spirit broad awake." Better be wakened at the cost of pain than drowse through life and die at last with half one's powers still in a state of lethargic slumber. "O Ploughman, drive the coulter deep and plough my living soul from sleep!"

There is a wakefulness that comes through friendship; mind is stimulated by mind. It was a memorable day when Coleridge and Hazlitt tramped the road from Wem to Shrewsbury. While Coleridge talked, as he only could, Hazlitt was "startled as from a deep sleep". His eyes were opened. It was the birthday of Hazlitt's mind. He had awakened to the fullness of life. There is a wakefulness of surprise: "An angel waked me as a man is wakened out of sleep." The angel of pain may do it; the angel of glory may do it. "When they were awake, they beheld his glory." On the Emmaus road and on the Mount when the disciples awaked from sorrow or slumber, they beheld His glory. Visions are lost on closed eyelids, they wait the open eye.

There is a wakefulness of final satisfaction. Death is a sleep but death is as temporary as a night's repose. We sleep to wake, The ultimate satisfaction, the crown of all our nature's yearning, is here: "I shall be satisfied—when I awake with thy likeness!" The earthly experience of the singer, as related in this psalm, gave ground for ample dissatisfaction, but his eyes were toward the sunrise of a better day, the day of final content when our God-given dreams come true.

ENTHUSIASM FOR GOD

" I will love Thee, O Lord."

THIS burst of human affection for God is one of the noblest utterances in the Old Testament. It touches the high peak of devotion, "Oh, but I do love thee, Jehovah," and then follows a list of names and titles that this lover of God heaps upon Him. And the list does not exhaust his emotion, even if, for the moment, it uses up his available language. God has done everything for him, God is everything to him, rapturously does he love Him for all His befriending.

The enthusiasm for God rests upon his experience of God in the wilderness, the deliverance God gave him in battle, the refuge God supplied in his extremity, the escape God furnished when he was hunted and cords and snares were laid for his capture; in his extremity he cried and God answered. If every effect must have an adequate cause, there is no human explanation of the fact that the cry of a hunted man sets the power of God in motion. Never did so little accomplish so much.

This personal experience of God explains or exemplifies some of the general truths about God, some of the principles He observes. With the pure He shows Himself pure, with the perverse He is froward. He saves the afflicted, He humbles the proud. To have learned from the struggles of life that God lives and loves His creatures, that He hears their cry and helps their helplessness, is to have gathered fruit in the wilderness and to have found a confidence that no discouragement can destroy.

> Lay hold of me with Thy strong grasp,
>   Let Thy Almighty arm
> In its embrace my weakness clasp,
>   And I shall fear no harm.

GOD'S TRIPLE BOOK

"The law of the Lord is perfect."

THE revelation of God is a three-volumed book.

The first revelation was written in creation; it is inscribed in earth and sky, in day and night, in sun and moon and star, in the rotations of planets and the seasons of the year; wisdom and love are written over His works. The universe is the work of intelligence, the deliberate plan, the considered scheme of God. If there is any restraint or obscurity, it is on our side. Earth's crammed with heaven and every common bush afire with God, but only he who sees takes off his shoes!

The second revelation was written in scripture, in the laws and commandments of His people. Nature does not make the same appeal to all minds, and God has not limited Himself to one manifestation. If the book of nature fail, the book of scripture may prevail. "The Bible is alive," said Luther, "it speaks to me; it has feet, it runs after me; it has hands, it lays hold on me." It is a book for all sorts and conditions of men. It is as varied as life; it meets us on the level of our thinking and brings us to the high plane of the thoughts of God. Christ is the heart and centre of the volume (Luke xxiv. 27).

God also has His writings in the human soul. We have His writing in ourselves. The poet asked for a more sensitive spirit, for clearer discernment of God's mind. There is a mysterious world within ourselves and in that interior universe are intuitions, achings, longings which require the experience of God for their satisfaction. Man is a homeless waif until he finds God, or yields to God's finding; after that he is a son of the House, and has the witness in himself. Nature, Scripture, and our own Experience combined to give us assurance that God is at the heart of things and all will be well.

> Thy purpose of eternal good
>   Let me but surely know;
> On this I'll lean, let changing mood
>   And feeling come and go.

THE SONG OF THE NAME

"In the Name of our God."

THE deliverance of the Name. The psalm encourages the king's expectation that the Lord will hear him in the day of trouble. No trust is here in man's prowess, no admiration for man's skill, only One is invoked. The name of Jehovah is used as personally as Jehovah Himself: "The name of the God of Jacob defend thee"; "In the name of our God we will set up our banners." The name is the means of His identification, it shows how far He is known and in what manner He is understood; here He is the God of Jacob, the God of deliverance for weak and sinful men.

The defiance of the Name. The loyalty expressed to the king and the devotion professed to God combine to produce the confidence and courage with which men wave their standards: "In the name of our God we will set up our banners." Confidence in God makes the timid heart defiantly brave. He is the God of the bannered host whose cause He champions and conducts to triumph. And He is the God of the lone soldier who must fight his solitary battle of the soul against the proud spirit of the world. David's untried youth was matched alone against the experienced Goliath, but he was unafraid: "Thou comest to me with a sword and with a spear and with a shield; but I come to thee in the Name of the Lord of hosts." This sense of warrant was nerve and strategy to him.

The defence of the Name. "Some trust in chariots and some in horses, but we will remember the name of the Lord our God." Cavalry and chariots are mightily real and terrible, but not more real than the presence of God to the devout heart. Israel had neither cavalry nor chariots like their enemies, but they had Jehovah, and He was greater than all the massed chariots and horsemen of any enemy of His people. His presence turns the scale in every battle, personal or national; His favour is decisive in every issue. Set up your banner in His name; set it up in school and college, in home and mill, in business and in Parliament. Plant His banner on the headlands of the world, and His truth in the hearts of all peoples.

THE PLENITUDE OF PROVIDENCE

" The blessings of goodness."

THERE is never any scarcity in God's supply. There is no rationing of His grace; what comes to us is only measured by our own receptiveness.

This royal song celebrates God's infinite mercy; God answers prayer, even the prayers of a king: "Thou hast given him his heart's desire." When this boon is promised to king or peasant, our first business must be the examination of our desires. The religion of Buddha considers Desire to be the root of all sorrow, therefore the duty of our lives is to eliminate desire; cut down our wants; cease to wish for things. But the gospel of Christ teaches rather the education of desire. It is easy for all of us to wish for wrong things; we are so naturally selfish, short-sighted and earth-bound that our primary concern should be to desire those things that God desires to give, being persuaded that we cannot improve upon His choices.

> Choose for us, God! nor let our weak preferring
>   Cheat our poor souls of good Thou hast designed;
> Choose for us, God! Thy wisdom is unerring,
>   And we are fools and blind.

God's inexhaustible liberality. He does not always wait for our petitions, He comes beforehand with His gift, "Thou preventest him with the blessings of goodness." He anticipates our wants, He forestalls our cry. And not only so, He surpasses our petitions, "He asked life of thee and thou gavest it him, even length of days for ever and ever." In His answers to our prayers God goes the second mile both in the gift and in the measure of it.

God's inescapable judgments. It was the business of the king to put down all opposition to his monarchy as being opposition to God's rule; the enemy were turned to flight, but the pursuers overtook them and so outflanked them as to meet them again in the face and complete their overthrow. When God's judgments take the field no wrong will escape. "Though the wheels of God grind slowly, yet they grind exceeding small. Though with patience He stands waiting, with exactness grinds He all."

FORSAKEN, BUT NOT FINALLY

" My God, my God, why hast Thou forsaken Me?"

THIS psalm begins with a sob and ends with a song. There was a gap of time and of experience between the two emotions expressed. The second part suggests a recovery of assurance.

The cry of personal distress with which the psalm opens is one of the saddest ever uttered in any language. A godly man feels himself forsaken of God! How easy it is to sing "He hides Himself so wondrously as though there were no God!"—but how dark can be the hiding of His face. This man feels that the God of his fathers and of his own youth has abandoned him. His depression overspreads his whole life. His contemporaries despise him; he is among the unwanted of his generation, but the bitterest cut of all is that God has turned His back on him. That man should behave after this sort was surprise enough, but that God should do so is mystery and darkness to him. Wonder steals his breath; he can only gasp his astonishment. The later part of the psalm recovers hope and assurance. "Be not far from me, O Lord; make haste to help me. . . . I will declare Thy name unto my brethren." Forsakenness was not the last experience of his life, nor the final word on his lips.

The cry of forsakenness has another history. It was the cry of Christ's darkest hour. He had known human desertion and that had wounded Him in the deep places of His life. The men He had trusted and leaned on to the last had turned away from Him and left Him to the devices of those who plotted for His life. He was not unaware of the instability of human nature. He knew its shifts and turns and limitations, but that God should do this thing reduced language to a gasping cry ere the solitary spirit sank exhausted into silence. The torturing pain of the slow dragging hours was overborne by the tense anguish of His spirit. This uttermost solitude of forsakenness is a depth we cannot sound.

The cry of forsakenness has been taken from us. We can never know what it means. So bitter, so mysterious, so strange was it that He would never permit His people to experience it, hence the renewed promise, "I will never leave you nor forsake you." There will be solitudes in the best of lives; lonely stretches of the road where we seem to walk alone, isolating difficulties and disappointments, temperamental doubts and fears; but His promise stands: You will never be alone; never left solitarily to yourself. Never for you the orphaned cry.

THE DIVINE SHEPHERDING

"The Lord is my Shepherd."

HE IS a mistaken man who seeks to be his own shepherd; only a little better by degree is the man who makes the State his shepherd, relying on his country for all he wants; a further improvement but just as unsatisfactory is achieved by the man who makes the Church his shepherd. He alone is wise who makes the Lord his shepherd; by such a man was this psalm written.

The divine shepherding is personal. This is the most personal of the psalms. It is *my* and *mine* and *me* all the way. "The Lord is *my* Shepherd." Robert Browning makes this discerning plea: "My God, my God! let me for once look on Thee **as** though nought else existed; we alone." So the psalmist, The Lord is my Shepherd as though nought else existed; we alone. It is the kind of thing each of us must say for ourselves. Jesus knew that one lost sheep will keep the shepherd from his bed until he finds it.

The divine shepherding is positive. It is the most active and practical thing in the world. There is no necessity overlooked or forgotten: God's sheep never lack; He finds for them green pastures. In every wilderness He scouts for the grassy patch, and in the lands of drought He knows where the springs of water are. He binds up the wounds of the stricken. He restores the weary. He leads in sure paths. His sheep are safely guided by day and securely folded by night.

The divine shepherding is protective. If, as may sometimes happen, there are gorges of gloom to be traversed, places of peril to be passed, His safeguards are so sure that His people have no need for fear. No enemy can deprive them of the supplies He provides. He gives abundant provision, His presence is pledge enough, the protection of His rod and staff afford His people constant security.

The divine shepherding is permanent. Goodness and mercy give His people constant company. The wilderness is a temporary habitation for the flock, but the house of God is a permanent dwelling; the sheep of the wilderness become the guests of His house, that is their dwelling-place until the length of days is fulfilled. Home are His people, home from the wilderness, and the pilgrim home from the road.

36

DWELLING TOGETHER

"Who shall stand in His holy place?"

"The earth is the Lord's and they that dwell therein." There is therefore no banishment or exile that can deprive His people of His company. He will share their dwelling in any solitude, and make common residence with them in desert or hermitage. But He does not give His company indiscriminately to the good and the evil.

Here are the titles to be won and worn; here the charter of the worshipper of God.

The guest of God must have "clean hands"; not conventional ceremonial, but moral cleanness: his behaviour must be above impeachment; innocent of violence and corruption, engaged in clean pursuits and wholesome living.

He must be "pure in heart"; his inward loyalty to God must approve itself to Him. Jesus said "Out of the heart proceed evil thoughts, murders, adulteries, fornication, thefts . . . these defile a man." "But lay up for yourselves treasures in heaven, for where your treasure is, there will your heart be also."

He must have "a soul that is not lifted up to vanity". He makes no concession to pride or pompousness, conceit is a spoiler, modesty is the acceptable manner.

He must be "a man of truth" who honourably recognises that his word is his bond: he must keep his vows with God and man. He is a whole man, singleminded, complete in his integrity.

These are great qualities for any of us to profess. If we cannot profess their achievement, we can use them as aspiration, as longing and seeking for their possession.

God Himself has His titles here. The procession moves towards the gates and the choir sing their challenge to those inside, to open the gates and swing wide the doors that the King of Glory may come in. "Who is this King of glory?" is twice asked and twice answered, "The Lord of Hosts, He is the King of glory." The hosts that belong to Him are the armies of Israel, the people of the Covenant, the inhabitants of the earth, the stars of the sky, the multitude of angels.

Will this God dwell upon the earth? He dwells with the contrite heart and the humble spirit; where these are found, there is His holy hill and there His temple.

ASHAMED!

"Let me not be ashamed."

A CIRCLE rounds upon itself and ends where it began. The prayer to be saved from shame begins and ends the psalm.

It is the petition of one who is sensitive to the opinion and goodwill of others. The things that shame a man are his defeats, his sins, his mistakes. What he wants is to be saved from his enemies so that they might not mock him; to be saved from his sins so that they might not destroy him; to be saved from false ways so that they might not lead him astray.

It is a petition for others as well as for himself: "Let none of them that wait on Thee be put to shame." He throws the safeguards of prayer around such as wait upon God; if he asks that those who forsake God should be put to shame, it is that, feeling reproach, they might return to Him. The Apostle Paul was not ashamed of the gospel, but he was often ashamed of himself for his misspent years and misguided zeal.

It is a petition for a safeguarded life: "Let me not be put to shame, for I have taken refuge in Thee." Our Lord's warning to His disciples was intended to safeguard them in the same way. If any of His disciples should be ashamed of Him, He would be ashamed of them before His Father and the holy angels. Not to be ashamed of ourselves is a good thing, not to have Christ ashamed of us is a better thing.

> Till then—nor is my boasting vain—
> Till then I boast a Saviour slain,
> And O may this my glory be,
> That Christ is not ashamed of me!

A LIFE UNDER INSPECTION

"Examine me, O Lord, and prove me."

HERE is a man who tells all his heart to God. He can no longer contain himself, but there is none to listen to his complaint. If he cannot speak, his very brain will crack. He must have a confidant, a confessor to whom he can tell even the last secret of his nature.

There is a life that he seeks. His one desire is that he might stand well with God; this is not a vain ambition, stretching his hand to the stars and grasping nothing but the wind. The serious undertaking of his life is to hold himself upright, to walk in integrity before God. The truth of God is the path he treads, the loving-kindness of God is the constraint he obeys.

There is a life that he shuns. The man who walks with God cannot adopt the ways and habits of the world. If the godly man will not separate himself from the principles and practices of the ungodly he will find, if he is true, that other men separate themselves from his company. No one was a greater "Friend of sinners" than Christ, and yet no one was more "separate from sinners". Christian people must do their work in the world, but their influence upon the world will depend upon their distinctiveness from it, as distinct as the leaven from the lump, until the leaven changes its environment into its own substance and likeness.

There is a life that he saves. It is by his devotion to God on the one hand and his distinctiveness from the life of the world on the other hand, that he not only saves himself but may save others with him. From consideration of the ways of the world the Psalmist more resolutely seeks a closer acquaintance with God. That is his fixed intention and final choice. "Seek first the Kingdom of God or leave it alone"; this was the constant urge of Henry Drummond upon his student audiences. "Do not be an amphibian, trying to live two lives. Be a Christian out and out."

SIMPLICITY

"One thing have I desired of the Lord."

"PITY my simplicity" was part of the prayer which many of us were taught to say in our childhood. "Pity my complexity" may well be the prayer of our maturer years. The British tourist has been described as a luggage overseer; he has accustomed himself to much baggage. We have much to do to reduce our modern civilisation to a simpler model. The Apostle Paul learned from Christ the practice and advocacy of the simple life. Consider this older scheme of things:

Simplify your desires. Wordsworth complained of "the weight of chance desires". This Hebrew singer is not troubled that way; with attractive simplicity he says, "One thing have I desired of the Lord." Most of us desire many things; we rarely try to find contentment by reducing our wants; that is a safer road to peace of mind than increasing our goods. The more our property increases the more our anxieties grow.

Simplify your possessions. The satisfaction of life does not depend upon its multiplied goods. There came to Christ a young man who was rich in comforts, in culture and in character, but the most significant thing about his life was its incompleteness. The one thing he lacked was Christ. Without Him all his other possessions were as nothing; with Him he could very profitably shed much that he owned.

Simplify your indulgences. Martha made life unnecessarily burdensome, but Jesus said that only one thing was needful. He was speaking of the necessities of life, not of its luxuries. If we lived nearer the line of necessity we should greatly simplify life for ourselves and for everybody. Christ lived on the plane of necessity, He was never cumbered with luxuries, and His was the perfect life, all glorious, all divine.

THE UNBEARABLE SILENCE

"Be not silent unto me."

THERE is a familiar saying that speech is silver but silence is golden! But that must be qualified. There are silences that are open to doubt. One of our poets freely affirms that many a lie is told in silence; the silence of cowardice; something had been said that was not true, but it passed uncorrected and unchallenged by another who knew its untruth and let it go! There are silences that deceive and hurt, silences that wound and betray.

But there are no silences that men have learned to fear more than the silences of God. And these occur not because God has nothing to say; His is not the silence of indifference. Longfellow has written of the apparent indifference of Nature. A ship goes out to sea with its human cargo, and the tide flows and the tide ebbs; comes night, comes day, and the tide flows and the tide ebbs; far out at sea the ship goes down, the seamen are lost, and the tide flows and the tide ebbs!—in a world of indifference, a world careless of human values.

Little wonder that a voice in ancient Rome cried out, "Speak that we may know You." Luther in one vehement hour cried, "Be not silent unto us; speak, speak, be it but in anger, speak, only speak!" Psalmists, prophets, reformers have confessed that any speech of God is preferable to His mysterious silences. If God be silent to us, said the Psalmist, nothing can prevent us from sliding down to the pit.

God has spoken. Christ is His word to men. And yet Christ Himself suffered the strange silences of God. There was a place called Calvary where Jesus was crucified, and God let it happen without rebuke or protest! Was it the silence of acquiescence or the silence of restraint; but far more than anything else, was it not a speaking silence, the silence of suffering? "God was in Christ reconciling the world unto Himself." Christ was God in pain, in grief, in sorrow.

The deepest sympathy, even on the human plane, is often a silent sympathy; feelings that lie too deep for words. The cross was God's last word in face of human wrong. His was the silence of unutterable things. There was no word sufficient that men could understand. The best cannot be spoken; it must be acted, and God did it. But His silence will not be for ever. He will come and He will speak; and when He speaks, He will be justified.

41

THE VOICE OF THE LORD

"Lord, speak to me, that I may speak
In living echoes of Thy tone."

THE world is full of voices; the ether vibrates with their sound. But there is a voice that does not need the ether for its transmission; it is the voice of God, the voice that speaks to us in our dreams and intuitions, in conscience and memory and a thousand other ways. It may be soft as the voice that wakened sleeping Samuel, or the still small voice that caught the ear of Elijah at Horeb, or the strong voice that tamed the stormy wind and tempest in the soul of Saul of Tarsus.

Consider the pervasiveness of it. I recall a wonderful piece of music, "A Storm in the Alps", played by the composer in the Cathedral at Lucerne. The organ seemed to repeat the boom and crash of thunder as it reverberated round the summits. It reproduced the sound of the wind as it howled and moaned, once muffled and then mounting through a snarl to a roar that made the mountains echo its tumult and its fainting growl. The psalm is the song of a storm. "The voice of the Lord is upon the waters, upon many waters." It overspreads the flood; it is as pervasive as the thunder, as outspreading as the sea.

Consider its power. "The voice of the Lord breaketh the cedars and divideth the flames of the fire; it is full of majesty." Some of our voices only agitate the atmosphere, they make a slight disturbance, a tremulous sound which is heard for a moment and then dies in silence, nothing else happens. But the voice of the Lord makes things happen. He spake and it was done, He commanded and it stood fast; the wind and the sea obey Him.

Consider how penetrating it is. It not only spreads itself out, it sinks deep in, it reaches past the ear to the heart and stirs the emotions. The Psalmist has said that the mountains and the forest and the wilderness echo to its tones. No voice travels further. Jesus called with a loud voice, "Lazarus, come forth," and he that was dead came forth. His voice penetrated to the regions of the dead and the spirit came back at His call.

PRESUMPTION

"In my prosperity I said!"

SOME of the things people say are the result of mood; if they are cheerful they say cheerful things, if they are successful they talk boastfully: "I said in my prosperity, I shall not be moved." His was a cheerful, confident humour. There was in his mind no sense of risk, no fear of change. "Soul, thou hast much goods laid up for many years; take thine ease, eat, drink and be merry." He said in his heart that he would not be moved, adversity would never knock at his door.

Some of the things people say are prompted by the place where they are or the company they are in. The Pharisee at the gate of the temple was prompted to pray, it was the right thing to do in a place like that. He found a publican near-by whose presence prompted him to give God thanks that he was not as other men are, extortioners, unjust, or even like the publican. It was the presumption of a spoiling prosperity. Prosperity frustrated the rich young ruler's quest of eternal life. His possessions stood in the way of his peace. Concerning a people whose riches had increased, John Wesley said: "I warned them in the strongest terms I could." Success and gain have their risks as well as failure and loss.

Some of the things people say are determined by their circumstances. The peril of prosperity is that men forget how precarious it is. When Job was prosperous he said, "I shall die in my nest." But within a short time the nest was destroyed by bereavement, suffering and loss. There is nothing more precarious than prosperity; if it does not leave you, it is very certain that you must leave it, and that may happen with alarming suddenness, as when the man of Christ's story considered himself safe and comfortable for many years, whereas he passed that night to his final accounting. He forgot that all of us live under the discipline of uncertainty. Rarely do we get tokens in advance of the things that are on their way, but we can dispense with tokens if we know that—

> My times are in Thy hand,
> My God, I wish them there.

43

THE SOB THAT BECAME A SONG

"Thou hast considered my trouble."

THIS man begins low down but he does not stay there. "My life is spent with grief", thus gloomily he begins; but he ends with happy gleam, "Blessed be the Lord, for He showed me His marvellous kindness."

The first comfort of his sobbing heart was his confidence in God. Before he relates his trouble he confesses his implicit trust in God as his rock and fortress. This helps him to meet his trouble on his feet, to stand up and take it and finally change it. This reveals his state of mind, his feeling about himself, his assurance that his spirit is in God's keeping and all the seasons of his life are in God's control.

The experience of trouble is half his story. He is disturbed by his own failures. He is perplexed because he finds himself avoided by his neighbours, disliked as a stranger, and forgotten as men forget the dead. To be despised, overlooked, passed over, shunned, forgotten, the target of bitter slander and persecution, is an experience not easy to bear.

But the experience of God's goodness is the other half of his story. He discovers that although he had felt himself shut up into the hand of the enemy, God actually kept his spirit at liberty. He learned to live his life from within, and that new secret overcame every sense of limitation and fear. God's enlargements grow out of our narrowness; the place in which we live our life and do our work is often larger than we think.

The expectation he cherishes is that God will come to his help; therefore great things are in store for the future. He will provide safety for His people, He will hide them where no evil shall touch them, no foe shall follow, nor mischief lift its hand. The man put his trouble into a prayer and then into a song and so got rid of it; he sings his song to cheer his fellow-men, to cheer them on to God.

A SONG OF THANKSGIVING

" Thou forgavest the iniquity of my sin."

GRATITUDE finds speech in this song of cheerfulness; it is a red-hot production, it is lyrical, it is explosive in its outburst, "Blessed is the man"; so he sings in his full and crowded heart of the forgiveness of his sin, and that is surely the sweetest song on human lips.

It is a song of contrition. There is no forgiveness without that. He had done something wrong and he tried to keep silence about it, but that wasn't any good. People suggested to him one expedient after another to relieve the pressure of his spirit, but these devices only increased his distraction. He found that only the confession of his sins to God cancelled them out, and when they are cancelled out the now unburdened heart finds living to be a gladsome thing.

> Though we forget You—You will not forget us,
> We feel so sure You will not forget us,
> But stay with us until this dream is past;
> And so we ask for courage, strength and pardon,
> Especially, I think, we ask for pardon,
> And that You'll stand beside us to the last.

Hence it is a song of encouragement: he turned his perplexity into a prayer and he emerged from his experience with a sure confidence in God for himself and for all mankind. Some poems are copyright, but this man builds no fence around his song, it belongs to "everyman"; all the world can get the same boon, experience the same benefit, and sing his song after him.

Hence also it is a song of confidence in the future. God breaks in with the promise that He will undertake for his servant, giving him the threefold promise: I will instruct, I will teach, I will guide. The search for guidance is the quest of many hearts, it is the theme and burden of many prayers; here is a triple assurance which will fortify all hearts against fear, and bring us all safely on our way.

IN PRAISE OF PRAISE

"Praise is comely for the upright."

"THE world is so full of a number of things, I am sure we should all be as happy as kings." In the number of things is the singer's *praise of the word of God.* God has spoken, He has not left us to guess His mind or grope for His way, He has committed Himself to recorded speech and the printed page, and He will honour every word He has spoken.

Praise for God's creation is included. By His word He made the heavens and gathered the waters together to a sea. These things did not happen, no coincidence brought them about, no fortuitous concourse of atoms grew to solid ground; God did it. The world we live in is His thought and His act.

Praise for God's counsel is sung. His word is not variable and subject to revision, it "standeth for ever". He gives knowledge, information, guidance, warnings against evil, encouragement towards good. One of the names chosen for the coming Messiah was Counsellor; with perfect knowledge at His disposal, He would be and was the teacher of the minds and hearts of men.

Praise for God's providence is in the song. "His eye is upon them that fear Him, to keep them alive in famine." Our human emergencies do not take Him unawares or find Him unprepared; they never outwit Him, never exceed His power, never defeat His purpose. Our lives are within His care, it is His doing, and that is enough to banish all our timidity and apprehension. He turns our nights to mornings and our winters into spring.

> A Song of sunshine through the rain,
>   Of Spring across the snow;
> A balm to heal the hurts of pain,
>   A peace surpassing woe.
> Lift up your heads, ye sorrowing ones,
>   And be ye glad at heart,
> For Calvary and Easter day—
> Earth's saddest day and gladdest day,
>   Were just three days apart.

THE ZEST OF LIFE

"Taste and see."

THERE is an Eastern proverb that says, "A man who has a sour face should not open a shop." Here is a spirit that opens shop and opens it with a cheer.

"I will bless the Lord at all times, his praise shall continually be in my mouth." It is not easy, it might not even be true to say, "I feel like singing all the time"; there are occasions when we are not in singing mood. Many things in this world are subject to their season, and are periodically out of season; but this gladness is perpetually in season; there is not an hour when it is inappropriate.

He sings the Doxology at all times, not only after the boon he has requested has been granted, but at the beginning, before the good he desires has been received. Nothing honours God so much as a reliance upon His mercy that gives thanks in advance and lives in an atmosphere of thanksgiving. How can we maintain this high level? How can we keep it up? The changing events of the world and the fluctuations of our own emotions fill us with inconstancy. That is why such hymns as "Abide with me" make their great appeal. We clutch at constancy and continuance, and are, aware that only God can give them to us.

The singer's abundant praise and abundant confidence rest upon his abundant experience of the deliverances of God. Repeatedly in the song he celebrates God's deliverance of him from all troubles, all terrors, all distresses, all straits, all afflictions. There is no exception to this experience; God's deliverances have overspread all his life, hence the fulness of life that overflows restraint and makes him bless the Lord at all times. So exuberant is he in his experience of God that he cries to all whom he can reach—men and women and little children—"O taste and see that God is good." "Taste and see." Try it for yourself. This is the very zest of life.

DIVINE INTERVENTIONS

"O Lord, stand up for me!"

WHEN a man's life is in danger and he has no hope of help from others, nor any confidence in himself, to whom can he turn for relief or rescue? The Psalmist in his extremity turned to God: "Plead my cause, O God, with them that strive with me; fight against them that fight against me."

It is a petition for intervention. He feels that his cause is to be tested in the law-court and he wants someone to appear for him, to undertake his case, to plead his cause, to be his advocate. This title was given to Christ: "If any man sin we have an Advocate with the Father, Jesus Christ the righteous." All of us have need of someone who will sponsor our cause before the eternal righteousness. During His earthly ministry our Lord repeatedly intervened on behalf of the weak, the oppressed and the poor. Have you engaged Him to be your Advocate before the final tribunal?

The next petition is for a champion to defend him in strife: "Fight against them that fight against me." David had gone out single-handed to meet Goliath and had won that contest, now he needed someone who would contend for himself, and he asks God to do it. Prophet and Psalmist agree in the belief that, "When Satan shall come in like a flood, the Spirit of the Lord will lift up a standard against him." But the Psalmist wants swift action; he complains that God is not in a hurry! "Lord, how long wilt Thou look on? Stir up Thyself and awake!" He is himself a stout advocate of his case.

The final petition of all of us will be that Christ will undertake our case against the adversary of our souls. And that will not be an isolated event; all our life long He will be on our side if we are on His side. Before Him every enemy goes down; His defence is surest safety.

THE COMPASS POINTS OF FAITH

" Taking direction from God."

THERE are four cardinal points to the mariner's compass, and there are four points to this man's faith.

The loving-kindness of God is as high as heaven. We know nothing higher than that, and it is a height we have not yet scaled. But there it is, overarching our heads and the whole world, the home of all our lights : the sun, the moon and the stars ; the limit of all our horizons. God's loving-kindness is like that, its height and its horizons are beyond our reach, they are always farther than our farthest.

The faithfulness of God reaches to the clouds. Loving-kindness by itself might be too indulgent, faithfulness is the guide of its exercise. The clouds float under the heavens and above the earth, they shelter the earth from the heat of the sun. The clouds dissolve in nourishing rain that changes the bare ground to fruitfulness, and makes the desert blossom as the rose. God's faithfulness is the fruitfulness of life.

The righteousness of God is as the mountains ; it has all the elements of loftiness and of greatness, it possesses elevation, permanence, sublimity. The Psalmist knew no safer hiding-place than the fastnesses of the hills afforded him ; he had known them from his youth, and they had given him safe concealment in the hour of danger and the day of battle. The righteousness of God has all these qualities ; the man whom it accuses will not escape, the man whom it defends will have no fear.

The judgments of God are ocean deep. The sea is the home of mystery ; how little of it we behold at any point of vantage or outlook, how shallow is the range of our sight, even the sun does not penetrate to the depths of the ocean. God does not explain everything, He holds much in reserve, He does not seem to act quickly ; the wicked cruelty of men and nations is allowed long life, but His judgments will not tarry past the hour His wisdom appoints for action.

The man who travels with these four points to his compass will not easily lose direction.

IN PRAISE OF PATIENCE

"Wait patiently."

IT has been said that worry is like a rocking-horse, it keeps you going but gets you nowhere. Here is counsel that sounds like an old man's mellow wisdom; he speaks out of the accumulated knowledge, experience, observation of the years. Three times he says you are not to worry. It is not worth while, as Abraham Lincoln said, to fret and fuss and get into a fever through envy or vindictiveness.

"Fret not thyself because of evil-doers, neither be thou envious against the workers of iniquity." His reason is that the day of evil-doers is short, length of life is promised to the righteous. If it be said that those whom the gods love die young, it is because those whom the gods love are never old. Worry and care and fretting age the heart, but trust in God keeps it young.

"Fret not thyself because of him who prospereth in his way, because of the man who bringeth wicked devices to pass." It is not easy to be content if one is eclipsed by unscrupulous men, and yet, there it is, "Fret not." Better is poverty with honour than riches with shame. Better a clean hand, however little it holds, than a hand soiled to make gain. Shun the wrong though a thousand practise it; follow the right without hesitation though you follow it alone.

"Fret not thyself in any wise to do evil." When you are tempted to copy the tricks of other men, when you are disposed to listen to the argument that others do it, therefore it is not so bad as it seems; do not compromise yourself, do not give good company to a bad thing, do not make your happiness depend upon prosperity. Do the right though the heavens fall. Be content with what you can cleanly do, and do not fret because it is little. It is never a little thing to do the right.

> Some will hate you, some will love you;
> Some will flatter, some will slight;
> Cease from man and look above you;
> Trust in God and do the right.

FROM SHADOW TO SUNLIGHT

"I am troubled . . . make haste to help me."

THERE is no shadow without sunlight; the brighter the light, the deeper the shadow. That is why the nearer a man comes to God the more he feels his imperfection; "they who fain would serve Thee best are conscious most of sin within." This penitential psalm breathes the spirit of contrition and of hope. If a man has fallen he does not require to remain in the dust; we fall to rise, to rise by the lift of God.

This man confesses the shadow of God's displeasure. When a man feels that God is displeased with him, nothing else goes well with him, everything in his life is disorganised. This man is troubled because he has fallen out with God, his sin has cast him out of countenance, the darkness of desolation is over him, he is a target for the arrows of God; there is no health or soundness in him, his life has gone to pieces, he is exhausted and crushed, he has turned blind and deaf; this language of affliction shows the sore trouble of his mind.

The sorrow of God's estrangement. The condition that he has so powerfully described expresses his own sorrow; no man can be happy who is estranged from God, or from whom God is estranged. "I have roared by reason of the disquietude of my heart, my groaning is not hid from Thee." The mistakes of his life have not only caused him pain, they have spilt his tears; roaring and groaning reveal his distress.

The supplication of God's favour. Three times he invokes the name of God, and each time the burden of his heart grows lighter. He begins with a plaintive cry to be saved from God's reproaches and ends with a life committed to God's care. The language of the psalm fits the lips of many of us, and when troubled man flings himself on the breast of God and finds peace there, he shows the rest of us the way home.

FUTILITY, BUT NOT FOR EVER

" Surely every man is vanity."

IT is an excellent thing to meet a man or woman who has no complaint to make. "I said I will take heed to my ways that I sin not with my tongue"—"While I was musing the fire burned, then spake I with my tongue." He was silent till he could hold himself in no longer.

The brevity of man's life pressed sorely upon him. Scarcely had he asked that God would show him the measure of his days than the answer came, and he exclaimed in reply, "Behold thou hast made my days as an hand-breadth." Reckoned by this small scale of measurement, man's existence upon the earth is but a little while.

The sense of futility accompanies the sense of brevity. The futility of man's labour laid its chilling sense upon his spirit, every man walketh in a vain show, he heapeth up riches and knoweth not who shall gather them. So quickly is life over and so futile does it appear, man's beauty consumes away like a moth! A traveller has written that, "Africa eats up time like a moth, slowly, noiselessly, ruinously." But there are other places where the moth is wastefully active, not merely in our cupboards and our clothes; in character, too, there are slow, silent, secret deteriorations like the slow decline of age.

But the recovery of his relish for life came swiftly to his relief. Short as it appears and futile as it looks, this man wants a little more of life than he has had. "Spare me that I may recover strength before I go hence and be no more." One of the brave men of Antarctic fame told the story of fierce blizzards and finished with the words, "Under its worst conditions this earth is a good place to live in." It is a brave word and a true one. The Psalmist's life has been hard and difficult, but give him a little more of it, the best may be yet to come. Believe that, and there will be a bridge across every river and stepping-stones at every ford.

A TESTIMONY

"Blessed is the man that maketh the Lord his trust."

WHAT does God do for a man who trusts Him? One man's testimony runs:

He gave me a hearing. "I waited patiently for the Lord and He heard me," that is the first great thing; a man's prayers are not words cast out on the vacant and empty air, to be answered by their own echo. No prayer fails of God's listening: "This poor man cried and the Lord heard." God may not answer sudden in a minute; He may keep you waiting for the boon you ask.

> How poor are they that have not patience!
> What wound did ever heal, but by degrees?

He gave me a lift. "He brought me up also out of an horrible pit, out of the miry clay." That is the elevation that comes to the man who seeks God's help; God takes him out of the mess that he has made, out of the hole into which he has fallen. When there was no ladder or stairway the lift of God rescued him. God does not stand afar off shouting directions to a man of what he is to do; He comes where the man is, and the man's experience of redemption begins there.

He gave me security. "He set my feet upon a rock and established my goings." It was not enough that he should be lifted out of the bog, saved from the morass, rescued from the swallowing quicksand, he was taken from a place where there was no footing to the sure footing of a rock. Security is the dream of nations and of men; it is the gift of God.

He gave me a song. Music was awakened in his soul, poetry ran through his spirit like a stream among the hills, his life had found its melody. What God had done for him was his inspiration and his theme. No man has so much to say that is worth listening to as the man who has had some experience of the love of God. For the rest of his life he is lips and hands and feet for the love of God.

THE DEEPER WOUND

" Mine own familiar friend!"

EXPERIENCE for most of us is a mixture; we meet people and we encounter conditions that can be helpful or harmful.

The spiteful had a share in this man's experience. He was unwell, some affliction had touched him, and his friends left him. The man at Bethesda said he had no friend when the water was troubled to bring him to the pool. But some of this man's acquaintances were even eager to see the end of him. There are always some waiting to share the spoil, or to find promotion and a place.

The unfaithful had their share in his distress; the wounds of his enemies pierced deep, but the wounds of unfaithful friends pierced deeper. When Cæsar was struck by Brutus, the blow of a friend not only wounded him, it deprived Cæsar of any effort at self-defence. Our Lord had no defence against the kiss of Judas. The wounds of friends who turn unfaithful fester to the point of death.

The helpful had a part in his experience. He was not utterly bereft; even one experience was enough for him to exclaim in his gratitude, "Blessed is the man that considereth the poor." None are so poor as those who have lost their health or lost their friends. But he found occasion to give thanks that, "In the darkest spot of earth some love is found." He found in God the one love that goes on when all other loves give up.

The true friend is one who comes in when all the world goes out. "Though all men forsake Thee, yet will not I," was the confident pledge of Peter; but he did not know his own weakness; no man knows that until he is tried. But there is one Friend who can make that promise and faithfully keep it; nothing can separate you from the love of Christ; He will stand beside you to the last: He will see you through. "All my friends are but One," wrote William Carey, "but_He is all-sufficient."

BOOK 2

Psalms 42–72

Wherever you begin to read in the Psalter you will not proceed far before you encounter some emotion that is seeking relief in language, some quest for counsel, some sharing of experience, some confession of want—not for bread but for God.

The Book starts with a picture out of nature that portrays the sore plight of man when God is absent from his life, or he is himself self-exiled from his God : "As the hart panteth after the water brooks, so panteth my soul after Thee, O God." The true comforts of man in every extremity of his life are with God. Man is made on such a scale of being that only God can be his salvation. God made him that way.

The Psalms are the most human of all the books that crowd the libraries of cities and institutions. Here you can see the defeats of men, the tragedy of human loss, the failure of man's best endeavour; here are his joys and sorrows, anxieties and hopes. He is a puzzle to himself: "What is man that Thou art mindful of him, or the son of man that Thou visitest him?" Here in this wonderful Psalter is his portrait drawn by himself when the passion to speak out his very heart would not be denied. This is not ancient history, it is the transcript of the mood and manner of human life in every age, and as much in our time as in any other.

WHEN THE SOUL SPEAKS

" My soul panteth . . . thirsteth."

THERE are occasions when the intellect speaks, when the heart speaks, when the body speaks, when circumstance speaks, but the deepest language of all is spoken by the soul.

There is an impressive naturalness in the illustration the writer uses, "As the hart panteth after the water brooks, so panteth my soul after Thee, O God." It is not always easy for us to hear or sense that inner voice of the soul. The noise of the outer world is apt to drown its speech; the clamant cry of the body for the satisfaction of its hunger and thirst is more palpable than the cry of the soul, but there are moments when the voice of the soul is more insistent than any other sound or consciousness; only we refuse to hear it, we put it off as being restlessness, a bad dream, an illusion, a sickness for which we seek a cure from the doctor and not from God. Nothing can be more artless or simple than the thirst of the stag for the streams, it belongs to the animal instinct, it is one of the first necessities of life. Every day and many times a day the necessity makes itself felt. Water is life, drought is death. It is with the same instinctive naturalness that the soul seeks after God.

There is an impressive intensity in the claim; something more than naturalness; a sense of loneliness, of being deserted, of being chased, as if he heard the baying of the hounds; nature increases her demands in emergency. William Cowper said he was "a stricken deer that left the herd long since": solitary, stricken, wounded; that intensified the thirst, the thirst for sympathy, the thirst for God.

There is an impressive confidence in the words. He reasoned that if in the providence of things there are streams for thirsty stags, there must be other streams for thirsty men. His thirst was not for money or fame, or pleasure or power; it was a thirst for God, and he knew with the utmost confidence of certainty there was a God to quench that thirst. On the sheer basis of the reasonableness of things, if there are streams for the thirsty stag, there is a God for the thirsty soul—"Ho, everyone that thirsteth, come ye to the waters."

DEPRESSION AND ITS CURE

" Hope in God."

NOT many of us escape those dark moods that are like night to the soul. Our lamps have gone out. Temptation, indulgence, sorrow or loss have quenched the light. Faith has broken down, hope has vanished, love has waned, and the soul having tried to grapple with its own trouble confesses with sorrow its failure.

Dissatisfaction deepens into despondency, and he interrogates himself, "Why art thou cast down, O my soul, and why art thou disquieted within me?" The cause of his despondency is his loneliness, the wounds of disappointment, the vacancy of memory; he feels himself forsaken, forgotten, the bottom has dropped out of things, the day to him is dark as night. It is not possible for us to put into words the "vexing thoughts" that trouble us; the doubts that arise from the new knowledge in the world, from the slow progress of good in the earth, from the recrudescence of the pagan way of life, the unmoral and so often immoral habits of men and women, from the wanton waste of war, and the mysterious maladies that afflict the innocent. Hope is a virtue hard to come by in a world like this.

The one means of recovery is God. He stakes no confidence in human assistance or relief, he directs his soul by one swift road to one sure supply, "Hope thou in God." In our blundering way we think of God last; if we were wiser, we would think of Him first, and coming directly to Him, the days of our sorrow would be ended. "My soul, hope thou in God, for I shall yet praise Him." The darkest night has its star; the longest night has its morning. There is a wind on the heath, brother; lift up your heart. All the cares of the world are not carried by one heart, they are carried by a million hearts, and are often carried with courage and patience and cheerfulness. Therefore, "Say not the struggle naught availeth, the labour and the wounds are vain"; say rather, "Your comrades chase e'en now the fliers, and but for you possess the field."

Here is what may be called Martin Luther's prescription for maintaining the zest of life: "Let me live as though Christ were crucified yesterday, risen today, coming tomorrow."

WHY WAS THE VICTORY LOST?

" Shall not God search this out?"

OUR own experiences often raise a question like that. When the victory was won, why was it not held? Was it not conclusive or was it disappointing? Why is it that something we have struggled to win, when it is won, disappoints us? Does it mean that the thing has changed its value, that we have failed to make an adequate use of it, or have we lost our relish for it?

The psalm strangely reverses its tone, it passes from thanksgiving for deliverance from the enemy to confess, "But thou hast cast us off and put us to shame. Thou goest not forth with our armies, Thou makest us to turn back from the enemy." Why does grateful recognition of divine favour change to the sad confession that these favours have ceased from our lives? Sometimes we lose our first victories because we fail to make adequate use of them, we become careless of the advantages gained; we forfeit through sin the favour that helped us. We alienated the powers that helped us and they withdrew their helpfulness. The loss of spiritual power is often insensible: "He wist not that the Lord was departed from him."

The final emotion is an anxiety to recover what has been lost, if that can be done. If one feels himself cast off, there is no reason why this should be the final state, hence the prayer, "Awake, O Lord; arise, cast us not off for ever." No loss is ever beyond recovery. God is able to save to the uttermost, and even that which was cast off may be gathered again. In answer to the soul's cry God comes to the rescue. Your life is not finished yet, there may be time to fight another battle and change the fortunes of the day. The soul that holds on to God is never finally defeated.

KING AND KINGDOM

"Things touching the King."

HERE is a song in which there is no note of alarm nor any sound of battle; it holds no whisper of fear, and makes no vindictive cry.

It celebrates the glory of the king. The immediate reference is to King Solomon, but the supreme reference is to the coming King. He has an impressive attractiveness, "He is fairer than the children of men"; He fulfils the promise, "Thine eyes shall see the King in His beauty." Christ had charm and an equally impressive authority. In Him doubt had no existence, faith was a singing certainty; "He spoke as one having authority," the authority of personality and of character; truth, meekness and righteousness were his adorning.

The description of the king and the kingdom runs into one. The character of the kingdom was determined by the character of the king. There are two things about the kingdom: the first is its eternal duration, "Thy throne, O God, is for ever and ever"; the second is its righteous character, "The sceptre of thy kingdom is a right sceptre." "Thou lovest righteousness and hatest wickedness, therefore God, even thy God, hath anointed thee with the oil of gladness above thy fellows." Our Lord confirmed and supplemented this ideal: "The Kingdom of God is not meat and drink but righteousness, peace and joy in the Holy Ghost"; that is the true sequence, righteousness first, the fruit of righteousness is peace, the accompaniment of peace is joy.

> If peace be in the heart,
> The wildest winter storm is full of solemn beauty,
> The midnight lightning flash but shows the path of duty,
> Each living creature tells some new and joyous story,
> The very trees and stones all catch a ray of glory,
> If peace be in the heart.

THE STILLNESS THAT IS STRENGTH

"Be still and know that I am God."

"A RARE psalm for a Christian" is how Oliver Cromwell put it in one of his speeches. Martin Luther had a like affection for it; for him and his friends it was a warrant for faith and fortitude.

The safeguards which these men and multitudes of others found in the psalm was not security against outward ill; they knew they had to meet besetments and antagonisms; not shelter from the battle, from the possibility of wounds and pain; it was security of mind they wanted, the assurance that they were on God's side in the controversy and the conflict. They accepted God's right to dispose the events of life as He pleased, and they made it their duty to acquiesce in His will.

Added to the security of mind they possessed was the near intimacy that God permitted them to have with Him. "God is in the midst—the Lord of Hosts is with us." Not afar off above the battle, but in it with them; not standing high up on the sea-beach out of the spray, but in the wash and surf of the storm, breasting the waves with them and they with Him. God will not consent to be exiled from any part of your experience; do not attempt to keep Him at arm's length. "In the midst" of things, that is where He wants to be; "with us", that is the partnership He desires.

Hence there comes that tranquillity men seek; seek and miss because they seek it in the wrong place and way: "Be still, and know!" It is not easy for us to be still; we are all overgrown children who cannot be at peace. But there is a deeper discipline and a greater stillness. "This is a heavy blow," wrote William Carey about the fire that destroyed the patient labour of years. "But I wish to be still and know that the Lord is God, and to bow to His will in everything." It was a great triumph of spirit over calamity. Surely its secret was the man's receptiveness of God; the peace of God that passeth all understanding gave him quietness of mind and the stillness that is strength.

SOVEREIGNTY

"The Lord is a great King."

THIS is one of the most jubilant songs, jubilant with accepted monarchy, the monarchy of God over all the earth. "The world is waiting for an Emperor," said an American to Dr. John Kelman who expressed surprise that a man of republican sympathies should approve of imperialistic ideals. "The Emperor is Jesus Christ," added the American in sufficient and confident explanation of his earlier sentence.

The sovereignty of God's power is here acclaimed: "The Lord most high is terrible, he is a great King over all the earth. He shall subdue the nations." His subduing power is ultimately irresistible, no one can contend with God and prosper, no weapons of man can match His weapons. But He subdues by love as well as by power. There is no instrument or weapon or force in all this world so subduing as the Cross of Christ; the triumphs of the sword are a trifle compared with the victories of His Cross.

The sovereignty of God's wisdom is also acknowledged: "He shall choose our inheritance for us." We have constantly to meet the necessity of making choice of one thing or another; in our perplexity we have wished that someone would decide for us, and tell us what we ought to do.

> I was not ever thus, nor prayed that Thou
>   Should'st lead me on;
> I loved to choose and see my path; but now,
>   Lead Thou me on;
> I loved the garish day, and, spite of fears,
> Pride ruled my will: remember not past years.

The sovereignty of God's holiness is celebrated; "He sitteth upon the throne of his holiness." His government is altogether righteous. The seer of Patmos had his vision of the great white throne, great in its unrivalled power, white in its matchless purity. The King is holy, His throne is holy, the subjects of His monarchy must be holy too; "Without holiness no man shall see the Lord."

IN PRAISE OF ZION

"Beautiful for situation is Mount Zion."

NEVER before in the history of Palestine has Jerusalem been the centre of such universal interest or the object of such frequent pilgrimage. Through two wars the troops of Western nations have been its encirclement of defence. It was my privilege to conduct the first Easter Sunday morning service in the Garden of the Sepulchre after British occupation in 1917–18. I never tired of the "three sacred miles" of the "Walk about Zion, go round about her, tell the towers thereof, mark well her bulwarks." The guide will show you a stone pillar that traditionally marks the centre of the earth. It may not be true geography, to many people it is true religion.

The dedication of Zion expressed the loyalty and affection of Israel; God was in it; His presence was its glory. It was beautiful in elevation, lovely in its loftiness, the joy of the whole earth; but its supreme glory was not anything of its own; the one fact that made it glorious was that God was there.

The deliverance of Zion from her adversaries was the joy and relief of her people. This was accomplished by divine intervention, "Thou breakest the ships of Tarshish with an east wind." The deliverance of the city from violence and her people from fear was an experience of God Himself. When our own country was delivered from the threatened attack of the Spanish Armada, the medal cast to celebrate the occasion bore the inscription, "Thou didst blow with Thy wind and they were scattered."

The delightsomeness of Zion gave joy to her people, "Let Mount Zion rejoice, compass Zion, walk round her, count her towers." God Himself was so sufficient a defence of Zion that her people could walk abroad in liberty and gladness. The experience of the past gave assurance for every other season, "As we have heard so have we seen." The promises of God are not words only, they are actions. His people's faith should be without fear and their joy should be an unclouded gladness.

AN INVITATION

"Give ear . . . my mouth shall speak of wisdom."

THE invitation is broadcast by messengers, "Hear this, all ye people; give ear all ye inhabitants of the world, both low and high, rich and poor." More than ever in the world to-day the anxiety of one place becomes the concern of all. The earth has contracted within the limits of one neighbourhood, so that a blow struck at one point reverberates through the whole. The human voice can make the ether transmit its message to the four corners of the earth. The gospel claims priority over other voices: "Give ear, all ye inhabitants of the world."

The call of God is an invitation to reliance upon Himself. The Psalmist complained that men rely on riches and boast of wealth, they cherish the expectation that their homes will last for ever, they give their names to their estates to keep their names alive, but man himself has no continuance; no wealth can purchase a single day of life, no influence can buy off judgment or death.

The hope of immortality relieved the rush of time and the threat of death. "God will redeem my soul from the power of the grave; for He shall receive me." The experience of Enoch may have been in the writer's mind, and he hoped that God would take him as He had taken Enoch; in this way he would be redeemed from the power of the grave. The grave is the limit of many human things, the rich will not take his riches with him. A few years ago there was an exhibition of art in London; "Death and the Misers," by Jan Lievens, depicted an aged couple hugging their hoard of gold while the woman vainly tried to resist the clutch of death upon her treasure and herself. At the last, death overcomes all resistance, and the summoned soul moves on unaccompanied by bag or baggage. Hold with a light hand that which you must leave behind; grasp firmly the spiritual riches you can carry past the grave.

THE BOON OF SINCERITY

"God is Judge."

IT has been said that sincerity is a virtue in decay. Human nature makes no secret of its guile; it is full of pose and posturing, it is clever in the art of "make-up". The game of pretending is no longer limited to the nursery, it is the common vogue of the grown-ups.

The sacrifice God desires is not merely an outward gift. With simple directness He says that He will not take the bullocks and goats of the herds; they are all His before they are offered, the people cannot give Him anything that does not already belong to Him. The blood of animals by itself has no significance; any sacrifice derives its value from the sincerity of the worshipper. The spirit and character of His people are His first concern.

The sanctity He demands is written in every line, it is supported by the severity He threatens. The people take His statutes upon their lips but they disregard them in their lives; they give His commandments the veneration of their tongue but they give them no place in their conduct. They do two opposite things with the same words, they repeat them with their lips but they reject them in their way of life. To those who forget Him, He urges a salutary remembrance, "Lest I tear you in pieces."

The salvation He promises is the welcome conclusion of the psalm. The hypocrisy that is condemned should be corrected at once, "To such as order their ways, God has promised His salvation." Men and women of penitent heart and rectified life are His people. He will not be put off with words, it is the language of the life He wants. It is not enough to say that you were converted once; submit your evidence, show proof of the experience; the converted man is the man who lives the converted life.

PENITENCE AND PARDON

" I acknowledge my transgressions."

THE confession of a penitent heart opens the psalm; without
introduction and without wasted word the heart of the man cries
for mercy. He confesses that he has broken God's law, that he
has missed the mark, that he has gone off the straight; his life
has gone badly astray and he admits his responsibility, he blames
nothing and no one but himself—*my* transgressions, *mine* iniquity, *my* sin. "Father, I have sinned," I did it, confessed the
Prodigal Son; without evasion, he took the blame, as all of us
must do at the last.

The petition of the man, made contrite by the realisation that
his sin was a bigger and costlier thing than he had thought, is
the cry that his heart might be purged, that his stained garments
might be washed, that the written record of his sins might be
blotted out, that the disease of his nature might be healed. The
language indicates the intensity of his spirit. God alone is able
to make his heart clean, to give him a right spirit, and save him
from being a castaway.

The intention of the forgiven man is that he will make known
the bountiful mercy of God: "Cast me not away, restore unto
me, uphold me—then will I teach transgressors Thy ways and
sinners shall be converted unto Thee; then shalt Thou be pleased
with the sacrifices of righteousness." The man who has been
forgiven and blest cannot keep silent about it, the instinct is to
speak of it to others and induce them to share the same experience. "With the heart man believes," but that is only going
half-way; "with the mouth confession is made unto salvation,"
that is going the whole distance. Share the good things, share
what the apostle calls "the kindness and love of God our
Saviour".

> Have you had a kindness shown?
>   Pass it on.
> 'Twas not given for you alone.
>   Pass it on.
> Let it ripen down the years,
> Let it wipe another's tears,
> Till in heaven the deed appears,
>   Pass it on.

CONTRAST

"Thou boastest thyself. . . . But I trust in the mercy of God."

THE contrast is between the man who boasts of the mischief he has done and the man who boasts of the mercy and goodness of God. The first hesitates at no evil if he can gain some apparent advantage from it; he is a man of false lips and perverse life whose behaviour provokes the moral indignation of men and the just judgments of God. The other is content to put his trust in God and await the divine vindication of his life.

Moral indignation, when righteously felt and exercised, shows a discriminating mind and an alert conscience. We are not always as indignant as we ought to be against many of the evils that blight mankind. The poet opens with an outburst of pent-up emotion, he is indignant because of oppression and treachery; he has seen power stalk forth in arrogance, he has seen malice at work and tyranny vaunting itself. Mighty men have presumed upon the loving-kindness of God, and because of its patience have taken liberties with the lives and properties of other people. Against this oppression the man makes his protest.

The moral vindication of the righteous takes two forms: it means the retribution of evil, and the recompense of good. Retribution will come as destruction, the wicked will be broken down like a fallen building, they will be uprooted like a tree torn from the soil by the wind, they will be laid hold of like a log that is drawn to the fire. The recompense of good will come to the righteous, they learn the lesson of these experiences and keep themselves from vanity and wrong. The goodness of God that has been abused by the wicked is the comfort and confidence of the righteous. Communion with Him is the secret of all fruitfulness and the source of every benefit.

SEEKING WITHOUT FINDING

"God looked to see if———"

SEEKING is an intensely human instinct; seeking knowledge and experience, seeking pleasure, money, love, friendship, satisfaction. Men have sought out new continents, they have discovered the gems of the mine and the pearls of the sea. But God is a seeker too; He is portrayed as seeking up and down city and country and universe to see if "there were any that did understand, that did seek God." He was seeking for seekers after Himself.

The divine sorrow was the fruitlessness of the search, the complete barrenness of the field. "Every one of them has gone back, they are altogether become filthy, there is none that doeth good, no, not one." This estimate of human quality admits no redeeming feature. There was not a single star to break the darkness of the night, not one flower in the garden, not one sheaf of grain in the field, not one man or woman whose direction was towards God. No situation could be more hopeless.

But God's resources are not exhausted: His solution is at hand. If salvation is to come, it must come out of Zion, and the eager expectation is that it will come; "When God bringeth back the captivity of His people, Jacob shall rejoice and Israel shall be glad." It is inevitable that human redemption should produce human gladness; it is equally sure that human advantage in goodness and truth will comfort the sorrow of God. To give Him pleasure achieves our own best peace. "Teach me to do the thing that pleaseth Thee" was the prayer that shaped a great life. Was it not the quest of the greatest Life? Does not that fact make it a pattern prayer?

> Thy wonderful, grand will, my God,
> With triumph now I make it mine,
> And love shall cry a joyous Yes!
> To every dear command of Thine.

PRESSURE TOWARDS GOD

"Oppressors seek after my soul."

OUR discouragements come chiefly from human conditions, from other people, sometimes from ourselves. Not once nor twice but many times, and for a variety of reasons, we get down-hearted. This man felt that circumstances conspired against him, people who disliked him sought to do him harm. Human enmities and human jealousies have often a persistent life and they make existence unhappy for many people.

If our discouragements come chiefly through human means, our encouragements are chiefly divine. As often as human things disappoint, depress or antagonise, so often does God come upon the field to relieve our distress, to support our weakness, to make us strong to endure. John Bunyan knew that if on the one side of the wall water was poured upon the fire to quench it, on the other side of the wall oil was poured upon the fire to nourish it. God's encouragements out-matched the discouragements of men.

The acknowledgment of the judgment of God is swiftly made; He will requite evil to them that lie in wait to do wrong, and He will safeguard them that do right. This man was delivered from all trouble, and immediately his spirit altered, his language passed from petition to praise. The rough road of trouble turned upon green pastures of peace, and the barren singer sang. There is no limit to the changes God can effect in us and for us. Conversion is not the one isolated event of a lifetime. It is a continual experience of things in ourselves and things around us being changed into something better than they were, so that the last emotion of life is not a sigh but a song, the final state is not blemish and imperfection but the spotless life.

THE DISPOSITION TO RUN AWAY

"I would hasten my escape."

IT is safe to say that for centuries men have dreamed of an age of flight. That age has come in our time and come with tragic consequences. "The human bird," said a great artist of the fifteenth century, "shall take his first flight, filling the world with amazement, all writings with his fame." The migration of birds is the instinctive quest of a better country, a country of favourable seasons. This migratory impulse is often felt and strongly felt in the human heart.

The pressure upon the Psalmist's spirit arose from two sources: the first was the enmity of those who opposed him; some people seem to be born to show dislike. The second source of his trouble was the betrayal of his friends; unfaithful friendships cause sorrows worse than death.

The inward pain urged him to change his sky; he wanted to fly away, to put a safe distance between him and his trouble. All of us know the wish to leave situations that are difficult, company that is uncongenial, duties that are irksome; we want to change our work, our neighbourhood, our country. The temptation to escape has tugged and pulled at many hearts. It has been suggested that religion itself is an escape, an escape of mind, a getting away from trouble by cultivating another set of interests.

Not many find escape without, but all may find an escape within, "As for me, I will call upon God, and he shall save me." "The name of the Lord is a strong tower, the righteous runneth into it and is safe." When you are tempted to run away, run in this direction and you will find strength and patience to win the victory where you are. If your flight is to Him, you need not leave the place that holds you. There, if anywhere, is your task and there your triumph awaits you; it is not the place that counts, it is the Presence.

THE TIME TO TRUST

"What time I am afraid!"

THERE are times when trust has a special exercise, there is a particular demand for it; it is the one thing that will help. The time of fear is the time to trust: "What time I am afraid, I will trust in Thee." Fear is sometimes the result of temperament, or it may be an apprehension because of uncertain health; when we are strong and well we can keep our fears at bay. Inward disquiet may make us afraid even if we do not always know the cause of that disquiet.

When some sense of spiritual depression overtakes you, when hope is dim, when some disappointment isolates you, when you have laboured long and have reaped no harvest for your toil, that is the time to trust. When life closes in upon you, seems to shut all doors and bar all gates against escape or liberty, you still can trust. So those six miners felt when entombed by disaster in a pit they scrawled on a door as their last message to the world, "The Lord preserve us, for we are all trusting in Christ."

When shadows overtake you and darkness like night descends upon the spirit, that is the time to trust. "Who is among you that walketh in darkness and hath no light, let him trust in the name of the Lord and stay upon his God." It is easy to sing when the morning is calm and the noonday is bright:

> I'd rather walk in the dark with God
> Than go alone in the light.

But if God is light and in Him is no darkness at all, how can you walk with Him in the dark? And yet if shadows thicken into darkness, trust and keep trusting, and hold on trusting still, and while you trust His dawn breaks through your gloom. The simple truth is, every time is the time to trust; even in the last extremity, "Though He slay me yet will I trust Him." "Though He slay me ten thousand times," said Samuel Rutherford, "ten thousand times will I trust Him."

A CRY FOR SHELTER

" In the shadow of Thy wings will I make my refuge."

SOME things are only done under pressure. We summon the doctor when trouble or pain comes to us, we seek the confidence of a trusted friend when perplexity disturbs us, and in our common life we seek God only when some illness overtakes us, some sorrow overshadows us. That is where the psalm begins; pressure sends the singer to God. He is a fugitive seeking shelter and he knows that there is no refuge so strong as the sheltering of God; there he will hide till the storm has spent itself.

The cause of his cry is the torment that he suffers at the hands of cruel men. They are like lions to his soul, he says that their teeth are spears and arrows. Among men he has been like one in the lair of wild beasts; jealousy and enmity and unmerited anger have inflicted sore wounds upon him and in his forsakenness and pain he calls upon God; he has no other helper.

The consequence of his cry is in his own recovered calm; the touch of God has composed his spirit, the danger is not over nor is it out of sight, but it has lost its terror; its teeth have been drawn, it has no longer any power to hurt. God is his refuge, he hides in Him, and in that hiding-place he hears the cruel winds and the baying of wolves but he no longer fears them.

The confident belief of Christian people, supported by many experiences, is that the God who delivered David, or as the Negro Spiritual has it, "The God who delivered Daniel is just the same to-day." Never was the word "Shelter" so much on the lips of men as in the days and nights of the sky invasion of our cities, and for many people the word became, in those perilous times, another name for God.

A BAD START

" They go astray as soon as they be born."

THE charge is made against the judges and the people that they are guilty of unrighteous conduct; they are perverse in every word. Their hearts are wicked; they start early, says the Psalmist, they go astray as soon as they are born. They are obstinate; instead of the goodness of God moving them to repentance, they harden themselves against it; they turn a deaf ear to His counsel, deaf are they as a deaf adder to his charmers; they are past feeling, they refuse correction.

All this dark record began with a bad start. The first right of a child is the right to be well-born, but some seem to miss this good heritage. These men were perverse from the beginning. A false step started a false pursuit, and they never changed direction. They persisted in corruption, they prostituted justice in the high places in the land, their ways were reprobate.

The petition is made for the frustration of their plans, that they may be deprived of their power to harm, that they may be like waters that disappear in the desert, rivers that have no continuance, arrows that are broken, and that everything they do may miscarry. The prayer is the cry of an anxious and agitated spirit, tense and vehement in its demand for divine action.

These experiences are followed by a sincere recognition of God. His activity, His vengeance will make it clear that there is a God that judgeth in the earth. The frustrations of wickedness are not because the wicked weaken and fail, but because the power of God overtakes them, causing their plans to fail and their schemes to suffer misfortune.

> Strong is His arm, His heart is wise;
>   Who dares with Him contend?
> Or who, that tries th' unequal strife,
>   Shall prosper in the end?

THE ASCENT OF PRAYER

" I will wait upon Thee,
I will sing of Thy power."

THE waiting heart starts the psalm. The prayer for deliverance
ends in the resolve to wait and see what God will do. The first
prayer is a prayer for himself; the Psalmist is in sore trouble, he
is the victim of unprovoked hatred, jealousy has mistaken him
for an enemy. He feels himself watched and waited for by day
and night; his adversary has sent scouts and spies after him,
they growl like dogs, they prowl at night like jackals, swords
are in their lips, their words cut like sharp blades. "They lie in
wait for my soul," and the one resolve that the soul forms within
itself is "I will wait upon Thee." Notice that balance of action:
"They wait for my soul". . . . "I will wait upon Thee." He
passes forward their evil intention for God to deal with it.

The singing heart concludes the psalm. The first part of the
psalm ends in waiting for God, the second part closes with a song.
The first is a prayer for deliverance from his adversaries, the
second is a prayer for the defeat of the adversaries themselves.
He does not hesitate to ask for them protracted pain and grief
and slow devouring. He judges that it will be good for them if
their penalties are prolonged, "for the sins of their mouth, their
cursing and lying."

The first part ends in waiting, the second closes in singing,
either because God has acted or because He is going to act.
Mountaineers speak of the singing level of the hills. Prayer is
the way to the singing level of the soul. We leave vindictiveness
behind us and mount to charity. We rise from the bitter to the
sweet. We ascend from scrutiny of self to surrender to God,
and are made recipients of His serenity.

73

"INTO EDOM"

"Who will bring me into the strong city?"

"THOU hast made us to drink the wine of astonishment." It was the astonishment of adversity, "Thou hast cast us off, thou that broken us down, thou hast showed us hard things." Life may be unexpectedly severe and stern. Things unlooked for may strike us hurtful blows.

That was the perplexity of king and people. They felt themselves "cast off" and "scattered". God in His displeasure seemed to have turned away from them. The very earth winced before His frown. The banner that He had given His people to be their token and pledge and rallying centre no longer served. The enemy had been too strong for them.

The second part of the psalm names the people and the part they are to play in the future; friend and foe alike.

It is a great leader that is wanted; one who will lead Israel into Edom, into the very city and stronghold of the enemy. Of Allenby, who defeated Israel's modern Edom, his biographer says: "Allenby had the strength never to look back at a decision once taken, either for pride or for regret. . . . The British Army has had few leaders less likely to lose heart in the darkest hour." The followers are many but the leaders are few; the lack of them gives false guides their chance to gratify their lust for power and gather the spoils of office.

The quest of leaders makes this lover of his country seek his answer in God. "Who will lead us into Edom? Wilt not Thou, O God?" It is a petition for the restoration of God's favour: "Give us help from trouble, for vain is the help of man." It is not the first time that disillusioned peoples have turned back to religion and to God. God's leadership will function through men and women who make it their business to be the brain and heart, the hands and feet, of the love of Christ and the will of God.

THE TIME TO PRAY

" When my heart is overwhelmed."

MANY of us pray only when trouble comes; "From the end of the earth will I cry unto Thee when my heart is overwhelmed." Perplexity is the great provocative of prayer. Adversity bends the knee that never stoops at any other time, yet our prayer is not unwelcome because necessity provokes it; He invites the emergency summons, "Call upon Me in the day of trouble and I will answer thee." When trouble comes, that is the time to pray.

The time to pray is as present and pressing as our common work. The task of living, the duty of making decisions, the responsibility of influence, the obligations we owe to God and business and other people make prayer-time necessary every day. Prayer, by the consent of God, engages Him to help us in everything, big or little, that makes up each common day.

The time to pray is when fear and misgiving overtake us; the profoundest convictions have their days of weakness, the strongest loyalties have their season of diffidence. Doubts and uncertainties discourage us, they weaken our purpose, they bring the clouds across the sky, they bring the mists athwart our way; that is the time to pray; pray the clouds away. It is mercy upon mercy that though we forget Him when things go well, and summon Him only when things go ill, yet He does not turn away from our distress.

The time to pray is when sorrow visits us, when loss, trial, deprivation overtake us. But the time to pray is not only when winter rolls the snowdrift to our door; it is also when summer makes the flowers grow in the garden, for the time to pray is every time; there is no time when God is not necessary.

Pray without ceasing, and with equal unceasingness will His mercies attend you.

EXPECTANCY

" Wait thou only upon·God."

SOME of the most revealing things in the world are the things
men say to themselves; the words may never be spoken, they
may be written in a diary, sometimes they only take shape in
the mind. This man said them to himself and then wrote them
down: "My soul, wait thou only upon God, for my expectation
is from Him." Write down your reflections; put your resolves
in black and white; speak them, test them by the sight of the
eye, test them by their sound in the ear.

He had been having a hard time, his world had been turned
upside down, evil had lifted its head proudly, the cynic and the
deceitful man had done subtle things to abuse him and to dis-
credit his faith. How does he bear himself in this situation? His
diary recalls his thought, "Leave it all quietly to God, my soul,
my rescue comes from Him alone." One of the comforts of the
afflicted life is that the last word and the final act are with God.
That fact ensures for all good things a happy ending.

There are two notable things here: (1) the survival of desire.
The singer did not yield to despair, he did not think that life had
exhausted itself, that existence was finished; he would not run
away, he would wait, there was something yet to come. (2) His
expectation turned to God. There is always the temptation to
lose one's enthusiasm for life, to indulge the sin of sadness. It
is a fine act of courage to keep confidence alive. When the world
seems to have nothing to give you, God has everything to give
you, therefore wait upon Him, let your expectation be from Him;
that is enough for all your need. But be sure that no effort of
your own is lacking to secure the thing you seek; the harvest of
idleness is an empty garner, but the harvest of labour is a full
barn. To the ploughed land and the sown seed God sends His
increase.

THE SOUL'S CONDITION

" My soul shall be satisfied."

THREE conditions of soul are here portrayed:

The Thirsty Soul. Thirst is one of the earliest human conditions; we are born thirsty, and at the other end of life one of
the last ministries is the moistening of the lips. Between these
two extremes, thirst sends us every day to the water springs.
The heat and drought of Bible lands make frequent allusion to
thirst inevitable. The thirst for God is as natural to the soul as
thirst of the body for water, and if there be water for physical
thirst there must also be springs of salvation for the thirst of the
soul.

The Satisfied Soul. For our common hungers and thirsts there
are always adequate supplies; these may not be immediately
available but there is provision in earth and sky and sea for every
human need; the world has been made that way. In the Gospel
of Christ there is power to save the whole world of mankind. In
both the natural and spiritual sphere we need to secure a better
distribution of benefits so that all may share and none may
suffer want.

The Pursuing Soul. The thirsty soul, now satisfied, seeks to
make permanent the possessions that have given contentment.
Hence the resolution, "My soul followeth hard after Thee."
Following hard means following close up, keeping near at hand.
Peter followed afar off, but that is unsatisfactory following; the
best following is keeping near to the leader, close up to the
commander.

> O for a closer walk with God,
> A calm and heavenly frame,
> A light to shine upon the road
> That leads me to the Lamb!

ARROW FOR ARROW

" They shoot their arrows. . . . But God shall shoot at them with an arrow."

THE language of pain is often a protest against suffering, especially against the unnecessary suffering which the cruelty of man inflicts upon his fellow-man. The man who speaks here is in serious danger, his life is in peril, hence the vehemence of his language. Men whose lives are threatened speak either with bitter vindictiveness against those who threaten violence, or with tender forgiveness because of the ignorance that commits outrage; men on the scaffold have cried for vengeance upon their persecutors, or, with Stephen, have prayed for their pardon.

The basis of judgment is clear. The wicked shoot their arrows at him, but he comforts himself with the fact that God shall shoot His arrows at them. The law permitted an eye for an eye, and a tooth for a tooth. The man had been sorely persecuted, his enemies had tried to find out something against him, anything for the sake of having a pretext for doing him injury. But, arrow for arrow, they will be met with their own weapons, "With what measure ye mete, it shall be measured to you again." What you throw on the receding tide will come back when the tide returns.

> You never can tell what your thoughts will do
>   In bringing you hate or love;
> For thoughts are things, and their airy wings
>   Are swifter than carrier dove;
> They follow the law of the universe,
>   Each thing must create its kind;
> And they speed o'er the track to bring you back
>   Whatever went forth of your mind.

There is a requital of mercy. Arrow for arrow suggests the other side of experience, "Blessed are the merciful for they shall obtain mercy." With the proud, froward and violent, God shows His sternness, He measures back to them what they measure out to others. With the humble, pitiful and kind, God shows Himself gentle, and recompenses good for good, kindness for kindness, charity for charity.

A SONG OF HARVEST

"Thou preparest them corn."

HARVEST FESTIVALS are a very ancient institution; this psalm was written for a thanksgiving occasion; the thanksgiving for ripened fruit and matured grain shows itself in gladness and song. There is in the harvest of orchard and field a sense of gift, something given without any idea of merit; there is also a sense of recompense, labour is rewarded; there is a sense of fulfilment, the hopes of the springtime are realised in the autumn.

The feeling of thankfulness expresses itself in religious worship. It would be strange if we felt grateful, but discovered that there was no one to receive our gratitude. There is no meaning in giving thanks to some impersonal power; one cannot intelligently thank the rain for falling or the sun for shining. These are God's gifts and they show that He is there; thankfulness for harvest is a confession that we are recipients of His favour, and that we live in Him and work with Him.

The feeling of thanksgiving reveals a sense of dependence; we are conscious of other powers combining with our own to produce the harvest that now makes glad the heart of the toiler. This sense of dependence is a persuasion of God; He is not reasoned, nor proved, but felt; this feeling is part of our religious faith. The insights and intuitions of the soul supply the material for reason to work with; we believe and then we prove. Even if faith is only a hesitating experiment, God will honour it, and if we are serious-minded the experiment will lead to a life-long experience of trust. God's rewards to faith are the harvest of the soul.

A DOUBLE INVITATION

"Come and see. . . . Come and hear."

"COME and See" is one of the first invitations of the gospel. If there or anywhere you are to see truly you must bring an alert and observant eye. "Come and hear" asks for a respectful and attentive listening. Faulty listening cheats many of us of things it would have been good for us to hear.

Come and See is an invitation to survey the scene of God's activities. Stand on high ground and let the wide fields of history bear witness to His power. On the great scale of the world's life, Behold and see, not nature only, but God, whose workshop nature is. We have often to widen the area of our observation so that we may see life whole. If we limit our survey to one place we may easily have faulty impressions of things good or bad; the wide field gives us a more accurate estimate of existing conditions. From the survey of the world the Psalmist turns to review the story of his own people. God was proving and refining His people and fitting them to be the vehicle of His message, the instrument of His power.

Come and Hear is a more personal invitation; the world scene contracts to the witness of a single life, "Come and hear, and I will declare what he hath done for my soul." The psalm begins with the wide outlook of world and nation, it ends, focused to one impressive point, in a heart fired by the thought that God has not turned away His loving-kindness from it. Every separate life has its claim upon and its share of the world-wide blessings of the gospel. As every blade of grass catches its own drop of dew and absorbs its own measure of light, so every sincere prayer will have its own answer. His loving-kindness will see to that.

That is how George Herbert sings of the refreshments and recoveries and renewals of God. They far surpassed his expectations:

> How fresh, O Lord, how sweet and clean
> Are Thy returns! . . .
> Who would have thought my shrivel'd heart
> Could have recovered greenesse? . . .
>   O my only light,
> It cannot be that I am he
> On whom Thy tempests fell all night!

THE WAY OF THE LORD

"That Thy way may be known."
"He made known His ways unto Moses."—Ps. ciii.
"Jesus said, I am the Way."—John xiv.

A WIDE and generous prayer is offered by a Hebrew heart, "That Thy way may be known upon the earth, Thy saving health among all nations."

The way of the Lord is an exalted path, it is described as a Highway, a way of holiness. God's ways are as high above our ways as heaven is high above the earth. His way is His manner of life, His thought, His will, His habitual action, His customary rules, His guiding principles. All of us have our own way of thinking and acting. God also has His and He makes it known for our guidance. He made known His ways unto Moses, His acts unto the children of men; the ways of His mind are more intimate knowledge than the works of His hands; the ways are personal, the works are public.

The way of the Lord is wide enough for all men to walk in it. The Hebrew writer recognises that it was open for all nations to use it. There is no invitation so generous as the gospel, its dimensions exceed measurement. It makes no exception; its appeal is without limit of language and without restriction of race.

The way of the Lord is narrow in its limitations, it is wide enough for all men, and yet it is so narrow that two cannot walk abreast. There is Another who walks with all of us, but that Other takes no room from the path, He lives in our hearts and walks on our feet. The narrow way restricts our baggage and limits our indulgences.

The way of the Lord was embodied in Christ. "That the way of the Lord might be known upon earth," Christ came, Himself the Way, the one way, the one way to immortality, the one way to the hearts of men, and for men the one way to the Kingdom of God. "No man cometh unto the Father but by Me"; He does not limit His introductions, for all who come to Him do by the same act come to God.

THE BEARER OF BURDENS

"Cast thy burden upon the Lord."—Ps. lv.
"The Lord daily beareth our burden."—R.V.

HERE is a heart that exults in the condescension of God. "Blessed be the Lord, our saving God, who daily bears the burden of our life" (Moffatt). This is the gospel of direct action. God is always with His people and active on their behalf. It is said of one of the kings of history that he believed he could conduct his campaigns from his palace, he could administer his kingdom from his study. But God is no such absentee. The difference between Him and us is so great and the gulf so wide that we could not come where He is, but He bridged the gulf and came to us.

See the considerateness of God. "He daily loads us with benefits"; this is one side of grace. One of His revered saints felt constrained to ask God to stay His hand lest His servant should break beneath the multitude of mercies too great to be borne. The other side of grace is suggested by the better reading, "He daily bears the burden of our life"; He understands our nature, knows our limitations, feels our pain, stoops to bear our trouble, to ease our hidden griefs.

The effectiveness of God enhances the whole experience. "Our saving God", as the Psalmist called Him, enters into the most ordinary experiences, shares the most familiar tasks, merges His life alike in the monotony and the emergency of our lives. His grace is not periodical, here to-day and away to-morrow, it is continuous, without interruption; it is saving, God comes to bless, to change us into His love, purity and goodness; "Blessed be the Lord, our saving God, who daily bears the burden of our life."

This hath He done and shall we not adore Him?
This shall He do and can we still despair?
Come, let us quickly fling ourselves before Him,
Cast at His feet the burthen of our care.

A SORE PLIGHT

" I am in trouble."

A CONFESSION of weariness is made in the psalm. Not many of us may share the tiredness which afflicts this man, "I am weary of my crying, my throat is dried, mine eyes fail while I wait for my God." It is not of tearful crying he complains though he has had much of that; it is of prayerful crying; he has waited long for answers to his petitions but they have not come. Some have confessed that they weary of believing, they want to see and know. Others are weary of hope deferred, weary of care, weary of the monotony that wastes the spirit.

A confession of loneliness is added. "I am become a stranger unto my family, I am full of heaviness, and I looked for some to take pity but there was none." He was ostracised, he found himself amongst the despised. His family misunderstood him and disowned him; there was none, not one, to take him "out of the mire", "out of the deep water", "out of the pit"; he was left alone, uncomforted, unwanted.

A confession of sadness shows a further burden: "I am poor and sorrowful." He was sorely dejected; his sorrow, his fasting, his sackcloth had been an offence to his friends, and their despising had broken his spirit. The judgment of those who had maltreated him would have relieved him with a sense of the justice of things, but his comfort was in the knowledge that the Lord heareth the poor and is the stay of the sorrowful.

The world wants more sunny Christians, said Henry Drummond. Self-pity will never make us sunny-tempered, sunny-faced or sunny-tongued. Open your life to the brightness of the glory of Christ; that will do it. He understands weariness for He suffered it, solitude for He endured it, sorrow for He shared it. Cultivate Him. His sympathy never fails, His refreshments never stale.

THE HASTE OF GOD

" Make haste. . . . Make haste."

THE absence of haste in God has been the complaint of men. God has been so apparently slow that good people have feared He might be too late to help them; and the wicked have presumed upon His silence. That God does not seem to be in a hurry provokes the impatience of some and encourages the slackness of others. "A day is with the Lord as a thousand years." He is independent of our measurements of time, He acts on the scale of His own.

The petition of haste is repeated three times. The danger is so imminent that the man has only time to cry out; in an emergency men do not study their speech, there is no time to choose their words, their language is a cry. The clock strikes out the little lives of men; time may appear to be nothing to God but it is everything to men, and its measures are swiftly exhausted. But the mind that fixed the limits of time by sun and moon and star needs no instruction as to its value. It is we who are learners here, not God.

The answer of haste comes speedily from God. The prophets of Baal cried all the day long but they received no answer because there was none to answer, but the cry of Elijah brought an immediate reply. "Before they call, I will answer"; this is the anticipating grace of God. He sees the inclination of our hearts, and before the mind can think the petition or the lips can form the words, the answer is on the way.

God answers sharp and sudden on some prayers,
And thrusts the thing we ask for in our faces.

AN OLD MAN'S PRAYER

" In the time of old age . . . when my strength faileth."

THE fear of old age is its frailty and its possible forsakenness; "Cast me not off in the time of old age; forsake me not when my strength faileth." There was a time when men and women were reckoned to be too old at forty, but the boundary cannot be rigidly fixed at any age; some are old when they are still young in years, and some are young when they are old. The fear is that when one can no longer maintain the excellence of his work he will be dismissed, and will take his place in the multitude of unwanted lives.

The memory of old age is often its best accompaniment; "O Lord, Thou hast taught me from my youth, Thou art my trust from my youth." God gave us memory so that in later years our youth should be renewed by its recollections. Select the things that are worth remembering, charge the memory with them, let them keep you company. Lamps lighted by the past send their guiding rays forward upon the future, giving us encouragement and endurance for the road.

The petition of old age is for a continuance of the mercy of past years. His enemies said that God had forsaken him, but he wards off this experience by his prayer; he craves the satisfaction of completing his work on earth and he hopes that God will bring him up again from the ground. He is confident that the years of his life have not exhausted the goodness of God, nor is God finished with him even when his earthly course is run. "Sometimes I am tempted to say, 'Would it were all over!' But I do not say it," confessed George Macdonald; "Let me be just as He wills, for His will is my will. Until we are ripe, it is not good we should drop; then we shall hang no longer." And when we drop, it will be into His hand. "If immortality were not true," cried Tennyson in the hearing of James Knowles, "I'd sink my head to-night in a chloroformed handkerchief and have done with it all." But the word of Christ calms all fears and confirms all hopes, "If it were not so I would have told you." Tennyson himself leaves us this better saying:

> Thou wilt not leave us in the dust;
> Thou madest man he knows not why;
> He thinks he was not made to die
> And Thou hast made him, Thou art just.

THE TRUE MONARCHY

"He shall judge Thy people with righteousness."

THE king's integrity is much commended and much desired. Tribute is paid to the uprightness of his character and the righteousness of his judgment. He will resist the oppression of the poor and establish safeguards for little children. Prosperity and peace are the accompaniments of his reign. In eastern countries water is the great worker of miracles, changing barren soil to fruitful ground, causing desert places to blossom and making safe the caravan routes in the wilderness. The monarchy is to be "as showers that water the earth". God's rain is a parable of the king's reign in welcome fruitfulness.

The king's territory is defined; "He shall have dominion from sea to sea and from the river unto the ends of the earth." The name of Canada was formerly the "United Provinces", but it is believed that Sir John Macdonald suggested the name "Dominion" for the United Provinces after encountering the text, "He shall have dominion from sea to sea" (Atlantic to Pacific), "and from the river" (St. Lawrence) "unto the ends of the earth" (North Pole). This is only a local use of a Dominion that is to extend to the four corners of the earth and embrace all peoples.

The king's supremacy over all monarchies is anticipated, a supremacy that was not gained by conquest but by personal superiority. "All kings shall fall before Him, all nations shall serve Him." Wider and ever wider in its extent, and enduring without end is the realm of Christ. Earthly kings have conquered new lands and lost them again; kingdoms and nations have changed hands and altered their constitutions many times. They will all be surpassed in the consummation of Christ's final rule; when He shall win the territories of the world He will hold His gains for ever. This psalm and theme inspired the hymn:

> Jesus shall reign where'er the sun
> Doth his successive journeys run;
> His Kingdom stretch from shore to shore,
> Till moons shall wax and wane no more.

BOOK 3

PSALMS 73–89

One of the great minds of the ancient world affirmed that the first essential to the ideal state or the ideal life is right ideas about God. Only when you have the right centre have you any chance of having the right circumference. Everywhere in the Psalms the religious element finds its highest expression.

Among other things, the Psalms reveal the struggles of the Hebrew people to reach clearer and better ideas of the Divine, and of man's relations to the Divine. The eyes of the writers are turned to God. To Him they tell their woes, confess their sins, seek pardon and help, make their complaints, offer thanksgiving and praise as the mood or need of the day inclines. Always a wistful yearning for a Coming One who would tell them all things.

The Psalms are radiant with the Messianic hope. "O that Thou wouldest rend the heavens and come down," was the cry for nearer and truer knowledge of God. When Jesus came the light of the knowledge of God grew in fulness: "I came forth from the Father and am come into the world." He was the answer to the cry of the dark and twilight centuries. From His advent and His passion come the new Psalms of a world gospel. The Son of David in Jewish relationship is the Son of Man in world kinship and appeal.

A NARROW ESCAPE

"Almost."

THAT word "Almost" is the key to much history, both of loss
and of gain. John Bunyan has told us that this word gave birth
to the *Pilgrim's Progress*.

> When at the first I took my pen in hand
> Thus for to write, I did not understand
> That I at all should make a little book
> In such a mode; nay, I had undertook
> To make another; which, when almost done,
> Before I was aware I this begun.

The perfect goodness of God is celebrated by the discerning
psalmist who is poet and historian: "Truly God is good to Israel
even to such as are of a clean heart." The goodness of God is
above question, it is beyond dispute, it fills the world of life as
the gracious light fills the day: "Ten thousand voices ever cry,
God made us all and God is good." There can be no controversy
about this.

The precarious life of man is contrasted with the perfect goodness of God: "Truly God is good, but as for me, my feet were
almost gone, my steps had well-nigh slipped." He came very
near to making shipwreck of his life, catastrophe lurked at his
very door, the calamity was only averted at the eleventh hour;
he was saved by the skin of his teeth. Everything was at hazard:
home, position, friends, prospects, usefulness, everything was on
the edge and almost over.

The perversion of his mind was the cause of all his trouble;
"I was envious at the foolish when I saw the prosperity of the
wicked." The inequalities of life embittered him, they clouded
his judgment, he was in revolt against God and the whole system
of things, until he went into the sanctuary; then he saw things
from a wider and clearer point of view, and he was saved from
false judgments, prejudiced opinions, wrong ambitions. It
averted a crisis in his career. This church-going habit of the Old
Testament and the New is immensely significant. Those who
practise it derive such advantage in the region of the spirit as
make it one of the great possessions of this earth. To go to the
house of God is as essential a part of man's nature as his going
to his own home.

THE OPPOSITE SEASONS

" Summer and Winter."

GAIN and loss are in the psalm, the gains that make life summer-like, the adversities and losses that bring winter to the heart. "Why hast Thou cast us off for ever?" cries the singer in his bleaker hour.

"Thou hast made Summer." Some things are easy of belief. When summer suns are glowing over land and sea, when happy life is flowing bountiful and free, then faith is easy, so easy that it is often taken for granted. The flowers are in bloom, the canticle of the birds is in meadow and glade, children are at play on the sea-beach, the soft winds, beauty and warmth, human health and happiness combine to say, Thou hast made summer.

"Thou hast made Winter." This is not always so easy of belief; winter has repelling conditions even if it has its white snow and silver mistletoe and red-berried holly, for it is the season when the birds are absent, the trees are bare, the earth is cold, and poverty feels the pinch of trouble; the winter of our discontent, the poet calls it.

> Winter reigneth o'er the land,
> Freezing with its icy breath;
> Dead and bare the tall trees stand;
> All is chill and drear as death.

"Thou hast made Summer and Winter." It was long believed that day and night and summer and winter were the creation of rival gods who had alternating periods of control in the earth. All the world knew which for the time being was victor by the conditions that prevailed. It was a new thing when men learned that there was one God over both conditions of beauty and bleakness; caressed with pleasure or chastened with pain. Not at once did they embrace the faith that He is good when He gives and when He takes; but these are two elements in one Providence and in one experience, both working out one plan.

> Men plough the fields and scatter
> The good seed on the land,
> But it is fed and watered
> By God's almighty hand;
> He sends the snow in winter,
> The warmth to swell the grain,
> The breezes and the sunshine
> And soft refreshing rain.

THE MIXTURE

"The cup is full of mixture."

THE cup of life is a mixture; it is never all sweet or all bitter at one and the same time; the sweet makes the bitter less bitter, and the bitter in turn moderates the sweetness of the sweet. In the hymns of the sanctuary we confess that all our joy is touched with pain, that shadows fall on brightest hours, that thorns remain, and we bravely try to reconcile ourselves to the mixture.

"In the hand of the Lord there is a cup and the wine is red; it is full of mixture." It was a cup of judgment for the wicked of the earth. Socrates drank the cup of hemlock that Athens doomed him to take. But our Lord drank the cup that the sin of the world put to His lips:

> Death and the curse were in the cup;
>   O Christ, 'twas full for Thee!
> But Thou hast drained the last dark drop;
>   'Tis empty now for me.

The mixture of the common cup of life confesses our limitations, as when Thomas Chalmers invited a guest "and told him with emphasis that we supped at nine. He came at eight and all forbearance and civility left me, and with my prayers I mixed the darkness of my own heart". On the other hand it makes admission of our dependence upon the aids of God for our best work; a few weeks after his ordination Thomas Boston wrote, "I was fascinated to my studies till the evening, mixing them with prayer." This way is disposition refined, and duty becomes a fruitful fascination.

There is another cup which all of us have to taste, the cup of experience; "it is full of mixture". Life for most of us is very complex, the ingredients of the cup are mingled joys and sorrows, gains and losses, and the one assurance that makes the cup drinkable will be the ability to say with the same devotion, "The cup that the Father giveth me, shall I not drink it?"

> And if some things I do not ask,
>   In my cup of blessing be,
> I would have my spirit filled the more
>   With grateful love to Thee.

SENTIMENT OF PLACE

"His name is great in Israel,
His dwelling place in Zion."

"THERE" marked the place of a great experience, "There brake
he the arrows of the bow." The intervention of Jehovah thwarted
the purpose of those who made war. He deprived them of their
weapons, He shivered their swords, He snapped their spears,
He crashed their chariots, He deprived them of the means of
mischief. Sennacherib was outmatched by the strategy of
Jehovah.

It marked a new strategy. Not on the battlefield, weapon for
weapon, were the instruments of the enemy broken, but in the
peaceful city and in the sanctuary. "There" the adversary was
checked, the teeth of the lion were broken, the fang of the serpent
was robbed of its poison. The victories of the temple are greater
than the victories of the battle. "There"—in the latter day the
nations will come, and "there" they will beat their swords into
ploughshares and their spears into pruning hooks.

It made the event memorable. History will never be allowed
to forget the spot where the big thing happened. Of all memorable
spots in the long, long story of man this is the most to be vene-
rated, "THERE they crucified Him." There on a rounded mount
outside the gate; there at the cross-roads where travellers, tramps
and hikers choose their way; there where the garden vines em-
bowered a tomb; THERE—that man's lost paradise might come
again—there they crucified Him.

It made the place distinctive. "There", memory recalls the
place made monumental by some experience. "There," said
Thomas Boston of the trees of his garden, "there I vowed the
vow and made my covenant with God." For ever hallowed is
the scene of some divine visitation, the place where some temptation was overcome, some enmity slain, some bitterness broken,
some deliverance granted from a snare. The place stands between
us and disaster. In spirit we take our shoes from our feet when
we think of it. It holds us like a magnet to purity and God.

MEMORIES

"I call to remembrance."

A TROUBLED memory speaks out its concern, "I remembered God and was troubled." The recollection did not bring relief; the trouble may have been accentuated because it added to his perplexity. He could not see a way through the mystery of providence but he knew that none could cure the troubles of man like the pity and patience of God. The top and bottom trouble of the world is that man is not right with God.

A grateful memory says, "I call to remembrance my song in the night." It is an excellent thing when memory is a ship that carries a cargo of cheer. Keats found "many delights on that glad day recalling". Memory had stored up some gladness that was available when hours of gloom visited the soul. All workers have periods of discouragement and unproductiveness, the poet's inspiration fails, the artist's fingers lose their deftness, the orator's brilliance ceases, but these pauses will pass; remembered gifts will come again.

A selective memory announces, "I will remember the works of the Lord, and the wonders of old." A poet exclaims, "Oh, memories that bless and burn." The memory requires training; you educate your mind, you exercise your fingers, you can also discipline your memory. "Those mountain climbs," said Dr. R. F. Horton, "and mountain visions have been a joy and inspiration all my life, and unlike the less striking aspects of nature, they remain vividly in my memory. If I were spared to see a blind and inactive old age, I could climb those great mountains and breathe their upper air almost with the same rapture in memory as I felt at the time." Choose memories that bless, recollections that inspire.

A reflective memory repeats, "I will remember the years of the Most High." We might distrust a single experience or an isolated event, but the continuous providences of year after year, the cumulative evidence of a long time is not easily refuted. The years speak with a thousand tongues and tell that His care is unremitting, His love unchanging.

OUR FATHERS

"God of our fathers, be with us yet,
Lest we forget."

IN this psalm the poet becomes the historian of his people. The whole story is not told in detail but enough is preserved to give the Hebrews the great background of their origin, enslavement, emancipation and homecoming. Their failures and apostasies are faithfully recorded; the mercy and goodness of God redeem the mistakes of Israel.

These are the encouragements of faith. The Ancient Mariner claimed that "he was the first that ever burst into that silent sea". The pathfinders have gone where no path existed, exploring the untravelled world. The realm of faith has had its pathfinders and we are treading the trail after them. "Our fathers have told us", for long ago the story was told by one to another until a written history appeared, the witness and support of faith.

The record is for instruction. "He established a testimony and appointed a law which He commanded our fathers to make known to their children." This is a narrative of experience; it is a textbook of history, still more it is history set to the music of words, a patriot's gift to his people, an illustration of the suggestion that the writer of a people's songs may be a better benefactor than the maker of their laws. Experience is something to be communicated, something to be passed on, something to be listened to by others and accepted for guidance.

But the communication of experience does not mean that it is only to be repeated in the lives of others. "I seem to see myself a sort of second edition of my father," said Thomas Carlyle. The true urge is to improve upon the earlier edition, whoever and whatever it was. We have sometimes to break the bond of similarity and of likeness, we have to make progress; build higher the fabric which our fathers raised, carry forward the story to new chapters of achievement. "Dwell not in the tents of your fathers, the world moves and we must move with it," was the urge of Mazzini, the Italian patriot, in the day that young Italy was seeking a larger freedom and a better way of life. The best is yet to be; the Kingdom of God is not yet but it will come. Go out and serve its increase.

93

AN EARLY CRUSADER

"The heathen are come into Thine inheritance."

THE complaint that starts the psalm is that the temple has been defiled by pagan feet and Jerusalem destroyed by the heathen. It was the plight of the sacred places that moved the soul of Peter the Hermit; it was repellent to his sensitive nature that the holy places should be the property of those who rejected the faith associated with them, and his preaching inspired the attempt to rescue them from pagan possession. Here the sorrow and humiliation of Israel's ruined temple and sacked city are the more personal and profound because the Psalmist is himself of Israel's birth.

The spirit of the Crusader is in the prayer that God will forgive the sins that had caused Israel to forfeit its inheritance, and that He will renew His favour and assist His people to recapture their lost glory. The plea for restoration is based upon the glory of God's name, because they are "Thy land", "Thy people", "Thine inheritance". If Israel is destroyed the heathen will not take it as evidence that God is just, but that He is too feeble to help them, too far away to send succour, too indifferent to care.

The promise of gratitude and faithfulness follows. If God will turn again the shame of His people to honour, they will themselves turn from their desertion. The writer is sensitive to the reproach of the heathen and he wants to disarm their scepticism. He is equally sensitive to the obligation of his people, it is their first duty to be faithful. The brave man makes this promise on their behalf.

"When wilt Thou save the people? O God of mercy, when?" may be changed to another and more pertinent line, "When will the people seek Thy salvation, O God of patience, when?"

THE VINE OF GOD

"Thou hast brought a vine out of Egypt."

THE past of Israel had its gleam and its gloom and it is upon these in turn that the singer reflects. He is depressed by the present state of his people. He recalls their redemption in the figure of a transplanted vine. One of God's first intentions concerning Israel was the removal of the people from captivity, saving them root and branch from Egypt and giving them a country of their own. God never leaves us as He finds us. The changes that He effects in our experience alter both our outward and our inward life. He changes both character and environment.

The transplanted vine was not left to itself, the divine husbandman took it under His own care. The vine-dressers were God's prophets sent to educate and refine the whole stock of Israel that the fruit of it might be pleasing in His sight. Isaiah depicts the defence provided. Without protecting walls the vines would lie open to the feet of trespassers and destructive creatures that prowl abroad. But He made Himself to Israel as a hedge around a garden, a wall about a city.

And then came Israel's lapse from faith and obedience so that God withdrew His blessing because of their infidelities; unprotected Israel was spoiled like a vine broken and trampled by wild animals, and the patriot breaks in, asking God to remember His purpose for Israel: "Visit this vine"; "Turn us again." The divine intention for Israel was that it should spread over the land, taking root in new ground and extending itself from place to place, destined at last to give Christ to the world, the true Vine whose branches are in all the lands:

> Praise to our God! the vine He set
> Within our coast is fruitful yet;
> On many a shore her seedlings grow;
> 'Neath many a sun her clusters glow.

95

THE DAY OF THE FEAST

"Our solemn feast day."

THERE are events in the lives of men and nations that are worthy
of celebration. Priest and people are here summoned to a festival
commemorating Israel's deliverance from Egypt. They celebrate
their freedoms—freedom from servitude and slave labour, freedom from fear, freedom from want, freedom of worship. If
Israel had remained faithful they would have been freed from
their own lusts and shames as well as from their adversaries, and
finest wheat and sweetest honey would be their fare. You say
this is poetry, assuming an extravagance of statement; but it is
the romance of life. He is poor who has had no festival day in
his experience.

The festival may celebrate some new departure in life, mark
the turning of the road, or the making of some new compact. A
man pursuing his daily craft found himself addressed by a
stranger who invited him to accompany him, and the man closed
shop and left. That night he made a supper celebrating his
discipleship; the man was Levi, the Matthew of the Gospels. We
do not know the name of the man who abandoned his home ties
and squandered both his substance and his soul until home-
sickness and want sent him back again, but a festival welcomed
his return, a festival that beggared all the revelry of his wasted
years.

Jesus made religion a festival, His ministry began at a wedding
and finished at a supper. The day of the feast is one continuous
day. Always the invitation is to a festival. He stands at the
door and knocks, and if any will open to Him He will come in
and hold festival, Himself providing the feast. His is a festival
of pardon and peace. Some captious spirits of the time of Christ
reprimanded His disciples for their gaiety; they commended the
disciples of John the Baptist for their solemnity and fasting.
Long afterwards their equally captious children said that Bunyan's pilgrim laughed too loud! Yet the New Testament, with
all its serious facing of the grim facts of sin and suffering and
sorrow, is the gayest book in all the world. "Be of good cheer."

WHEN JUDGES ARE JUDGED

"How long will ye judge unjustly?"

THAT land is in a poor state whose administrators and judges fail to hold the scales of justice even, who accept bribes, who indulge in partiality, prejudice, favour.

The divine solicitude is revealed by God's presence among the judges of Israel. They may have the last word in earthly counsel, but there is another tribunal before which they themselves must stand. God takes the judges to task for their unjust exercise of their office, protesting against their abuse of their privilege, taking the line of least resistance, persecuting and dealing harshly with those over whom their position gives them power. The divine protest urges the defence of the poor, the deliverance of the righteous, the saving of the needy.

The divine sorrow is that the protest made against unjust judgment is unavailing, it makes no difference, men have hardened their hearts against Him and are content to enjoy their own safety and comfort regardless of the ill-fortune of those who suffer at their hands and have none to take their part; those who should be the defence of the humble are their persecutors.

The divine succour is invited for them; if men fail to show pity, let God do so; if men have no righteousness, let God show himself righteous; His grace extends over all the earth and His power over the nations, let Him take the authority that is His and use it for the good of the people; let Him assert Himself and not keep silent, but deliver the righteous from the prejudice and persecution of unrighteous men.

WITH ONE CONSENT

" They have consulted together with one consent."

It has been said that there is no unity like a common enmity. The enemies of Israel had fought against one another, but when Israel was regarded as the common foe they fought as a united army "with one consent". Ten names are given of the hostile tribes that formed a league against Israel; their object was the complete destruction of Israel as a nation. People who have no love for one another come together under pressure to oppose some common adversary or protect some common interest. Herod and Pilate had been estranged but they were made friends by their common enmity against Christ.

There are common elements that reveal themselves without any agreement of policy or action, without any actual intention to act together. Jesus told of a supper having been prepared and when the guests who had been forewarned were sent for, they all "with one consent" began to make excuse. Each acted by himself, but their unwitting identity of conduct threatened to leave the banquet without guests. Our actions often give us strange company. They relate us to groups and factions from whom at other times we would turn swiftly away.

When Stephen was stoned, Saul of Tarsus stood by consenting to his death. Consent may be spoken or unspoken, a nod may be sufficient, a look may declare our faith or unfaith, our loyalty or disloyalty. "Madam, consent to go with Him," wrote Samuel Rutherford to Lady Kenmure. Give your consent to Christ; hold hard by Him. Take His side with the consent of all your powers, your life a united whole, wholly for Christ.

THE ENJOYMENT OF GOD

"O Lord of hosts, happy is the man that trusteth in Thee."

IT was said of John Buchan that the key to his life was Enjoyment. He enjoyed life, he enjoyed work, he enjoyed responsibility, he enjoyed his faith in God. He made personal the general principle that "Man's chief end is to glorify God and to enjoy Him for ever."

That happiness, that enjoyment is the possession of those whose security is in God. Sparrows and swallows making their nests in the eaves of the temple were the envy of one who coveted their privilege. But the dwelling-place of human nesting is not in anything material. "Build your nest in no tree here, for God hath committed the whole forest to death," wrote Samuel Rutherford. "I saw myself in my nest at Simprin," said Thomas Boston; but the nest was sorely disturbed. "I shall die in my nest," said Job in his prosperity, but the nest was shattered. Not anywhere but in the heart of God is there safe nesting.

It is the possession of those whose strength is in God. "It is a miserable thing to be weak," said Milton. It is a great thing to be strong, but what strength is there that is not at last the prey of weakness? The rocks crumble and the mountains decay, human strength fails and grey hairs appear, only the strength that is in God waxes more and more; the outward man perishes but the inward man is renewed day by day.

It is the possession of those whose serenity is in God. He is sun and shield to His people; He tempers all His providences and will not suffer you to be overborne. He stands between you and the storm; the evils of the world can have no power except by His permission; the shelter of His shield is your protection, He will hide you safely until the storms of life and death are overpast. Your life is hid with Christ in God—with Christ—in God. What hostile power can reach you there? Rest in that serenity.

> O Lord, how happy should we be
> If we could cast our care on Thee,
>   If we from self could rest,
> And feel at heart that One above,
> In perfect wisdom, perfect love,
>   Is working for the best.

LISTENING-IN

"I will hear what God has to say."

THE captivity of Israel is past, the exile is over and the liberated captives give thanks that God has broken their bondage and restored them to their own land. "Thou hast turned Thyself from Thy fierce anger," says the singer, and to match this experience from the human side he asks, "Turn us, O God of our salvation." The two turnings balance out and complete the event: what he wants for his people is their turning from the sins that were their former shame. Resolutely does the man turn attentively to God and to God alone.

More voices are speaking to the world to-day than ever before in its history, and reaching larger audiences than ever could assemble in one place. The voices that reach us are a chorus: the leaders of parties and of policies offer us chaotic counsel, each attempting to outspeak the rest. Are there many who listen-in here?—"I will hear what God the Lord will speak." It is a deliberate withdrawal from the loud voices and confused tongues of the earth:

> Oh, hush the noise, ye men of strife,
> And hear the angels sing.

It is as deliberate a withdrawal of attention from the language of one's own life:

> O let me hear Thee speaking In accents clear and still,
> Above the storms of passion, The murmurs of self-will.

If you have a discriminating ear you may hear Him in the open:

> Thy voice is on the rolling air,
> I hear Thee where the waters run.

If you listen in the temple you may, like Samuel, hear Him call you by your name, or you may hear Him ask for a volunteer as did Isaiah; you may hear His voice in your own house as was the experience of Ezekiel. If you have not heard His voice, has the listening been wrong?

> O speak to reassure me, To hasten or control;
> O speak, and make me listen, Thou Guardian of my soul.

TOKENS

" Show me a token for good."

It seems a natural thing for a man who seeks God's face to offer reasons why God should hear him. The Pharisee may suggest that his virtues merit God's attention: the Publican can only beg God's merciful interest in his case. Through various reasons of poverty and necessity he mounts to ask for some token of good.

The desire for some outward support of inward trust has been cherished in every generation. "Show me a token for good," was the prayer of the man who in his own time and for his own task desired some confirming evidence from God; not something to gratify his curiosity, but something to show in support of his faith; he wanted it for his own sake and for the sake of others that they too might believe.

Our Lord encountered repeated petitions for some sign or token of Himself. His miracles were intended to make faith easy, but in the ultimate He was Himself His own best token, "He that hath seen me hath seen the Father." He urged that the people had Moses and the prophets; if they did not believe them, neither would they believe though one rose from the dead. The Scriptures were to Christ's mind a reasonable and perpetual support of faith.

The supreme answer to the petition was given in the Upper Room, "He showed them His hands and His side; then were the disciples glad when they saw the Lord." When our sense of sin, our bitter regrets and our oppressive glooms disturb our hope, there is always His token, the mark of His wounds, the sign of His cross, to give us confidence and peace.

> Hath He marks to lead me to Him,
>   If He be my Guide?
> In His feet and hands are wound-prints,
>   And His side.

THE MOTHERHOOD OF ZION

"This and that man was born in her."

THE choice of Zion as the early centre of worship in Israel was God's own selection. The temple of Zion was built and wrecked, and built and wrecked again, but the significance was not so much in the place as in the faith that was proclaimed there. Zion was the habitation of the Presence, the seat of divine government, the shrine of divine worship. "Begin at Jerusalem," said our Lord, making Zion the originating centre of the gospel.

The attractiveness of Zion explains its reputation: "Glorious things are spoken of thee, O city of God."

> Glorious things of thee are spoken,
> Zion, city of our God;
> He whose word cannot be broken
> Formed thee for His own abode.
> On the Rock of Ages founded,
> What can shake thy sure repose?
> With salvation's walls surrounded,
> Thou may'st smile at all thy foes.

The faith that emanated from Zion was to go out to gather to itself the former enemies of Israel and make them friends; the pagan peoples were to become citizens enjoying equal rights with Israel. The faith of Christ is not the exclusive privilege of any people, it is the redeeming possession of all the world.

The record of Zion is kept by God Himself; He does not give the keeping of the citizen roll to any official of church or state. He keeps His own book of remembrance; in His book of life He writes the names with His own hand, and He counts His people as a shepherd counts his sheep. Saints, apostles, prophets, martyrs, the humble and true of every age are written in the book of God. The record of Zion is the roll-book of heaven. "To be mentioned in a book is part of immortality," wrote George Matheson. To be mentioned in the Book of Life is immortality itself:

> Saviour, if of Zion's city,
> I, through grace, a member am,
> Let the world deride or pity
> I will glory in Thy name.

DEGREES OF FELLOWSHIP

"Lover and Friend and Acquaintance."

HEAVIEST among the losses that grieved the singer was the loss of his kinships; "Lover and friend hast Thou put far from me, and mine acquaintance into darkness." There is something here to hold on to! It is an interesting assessment.

The psalm is a lament rather than a celebration, a sob rather than a song: "I have cried day and night—for my soul is full of troubles." This cry of a derelict life helps us to assess our human relationships.

There are degrees of intimacy. First and most numerous are our acquaintances; within this circle one life does not touch another very closely, there is no sharing of the inner things of the mind or the deeper things of experience. Next is the circle of friends; here acquaintance ripens into a considerable degree of trust and affection. But there is a smaller group, the few who may be called lovers. The scale of intimacy is like the tapering of a mountain; from the many acquaintances around the base the number thins through several friendships to the few lovers who can stand upon the summit.

There are corresponding degrees of devotion. There are many who have a remote acquaintance with God and Jesus Christ, they have some vague conception about who and what God is, who and what Christ is, but nothing beyond that. There are others who stand within an inner circle and are friends of Christ, they have a certain intimacy, they are on speaking terms, and have some measure of reverence and of regard. But the closest group of all is the company of the lovers of Christ. We can pass from one group to another as Peter passed from acquaintance to friendship, from friendship to loving; love was and is the perpetual bond. Your Lover in chief is Jesus Christ; that is the great word in the hymn, "Jesus, Lover of my soul". To love and be loved by another is a great part of life; to love and be loved by Him is the whole of life for ever and ever, and every other love is nobler because His is first.

THE DISCOVERY OF GOD

"I have found My servant."

THE divine search for some life that would serve the purpose of God achieved this success: "I have exalted one chosen out of the people. I have found David, My servant." Clifton Gateway at Niagara commemorates men and women who braved the wilderness, hewed their timber, built their huts, maintained the settlements and opened a way for civilisation. This is inscribed above the archway, "I sought for a man that should make up the hedge and stand in the gap for the land." The discovery of the man is the theme of God and of the gospel. "When God would save mankind," said Richard Baxter, "He did it by way of a Man."

The divine choice often falls upon apparently unlikely men. David was not Samuel's choice but he was God's, called from shepherding to monarchy. The divine search is often conducted in unlikely places. He found David among the sheepfolds as afterwards He found Livingstone in a factory, Mary Slessor in a mill, William Carey cobbling shoes, John Bunyan tinkering; the greatest drama of all was Christ of the cattle-shed and the carpenter's shop.

The divine elevations are an equal astonishment, no one but God could have thought of Saul of Tarsus for the vacancy in the apostleship. God's promotions do not end here; there are thrones waiting in the other world and fishermen out of Galilee will sit upon them, thrones whose glory far surpasses the most brilliant thrones this world has ever seen. The divine quest is not finished. Be ready for the summons and take it when it comes. Volunteer for it in advance; let Him know that you are prepared for anything He thinks you can be and do.

The motto of the Paratroop Regiment in British arms is *Utrinque Paratus*: Prepared for anything. It expresses gallant devotion; service without conditions. David Livingstone anticipated this high-spirited loyalty, "I will go anywhere, so long as it is forward." God had found His servant.

BOOK 4

PSALMS 90–106

The division of the Psalter into five books does not mean
that each is complete in itself or in its treatment of any great
doctrine or law. Some are prayers, some are thanksgivings,
some are praises that rise out of gratitude for personal and
national providences in times of stress; some are historical,
some are of the nature of instruction, others express hopes of
things to come.

The great word of the past and the prospect of the future
was the mercy that God had shown to Israel. The first name
by which God revealed Himself was, "I am the Lord Thy
God, Merciful and Gracious." It celebrates survival after
some great crisis: "It is of the Lord's mercy that we are not
consumed." It expresses triumph over fear or disaster: "I
will sing of the mercy of the Lord for ever."

Mercy is the great resounding word, and the persistent
experience of Israel. It anticipates the full and varied use
which the gospels make of it. "Have mercy on my son",
"Have mercy on my daughter", "Have mercy on me",
"God be merciful to me a sinner", so run the petitions of the
new age, summed up in the apostle's master appeal, "I
beseech you by the mercies of God." In them the Israel of
yesterday and the world of today have learned what God is
like.

LIFE OF GOD AND LIFE OF MAN

" A thousand years are but as yesterday."

THE eternity of God finds convinced expression. He is from ever-lasting to everlasting. To help the mind to some idea of perma-nence the writer fixes on the mountains. They are the oldest thing within our ken. The scars on the mountain face are the wrinkles of time. But God was before the mountains, and He will be there when the mountains have ceased to be. He is the one Permanence and the one Providence in all this world of flux and change. A thousand years are but a day in His eternity.

The brevity of man makes its confession. The frailty of human life is written in a variety of figures. It is like a river in swift flow, here for a moment then gone to the sea; it is cut down like grass after a few days' growth; it is a tale told and then for-gotten; it is a sigh, a momentary breath and then it is finished and all is over! The spirit within clutches at some hope of con-tinuance, some abiding. But there is also confession of the iniquity of life; "our sins", "our secret sins", "our iniquities". God alone is a match for all our disabilities and disqualifications.

> The period of life is brief,
> It is the red in the red rose leaf;
> It is the gold in the sunset sky;
> It is the flight of a bird on high;
> But one may fill the space
> With such an infinite grace,
> That the red shall vein all time,
> And the gold through the ages shine,
> And the bird fly swift and straight
> To the portals of God's own gate.

The brevity of man is garnered in the eternity of God; the iniquity of man is purged in the pity of God. Man's sinfulness accentuates the frailty and failure of his life; his sin is the cause of his sorrow because it deprived him of the fellowship of God. He calls upon God to return to him, to come back in pity and save his life from dust and his labour from nothingness. If our life is to be preserved, if our work is to have any permanence, God must approve and establish it, and build it into His scheme of things.

> We men, who in our morn of youth defied
> The elements, must vanish—be it so!
> Enough, if something from our hands have power
> To live, and act, and serve the future hour.

THE SECRET PLACE

"He that dwelleth in the secret place of the Most High."

THERE is intimate communion in the secret place. The perils of man and the protections of God are here the twin subjects of concern. There are many adversaries, there are snares, pestilences, terrors, arrows, destructions; they reveal a world that is thick with danger, but there is promised security for those who dwell in the secret place with God. In His company are the true safeguards of our life. He makes Himself a sheltering shadow to us, a secure fortress, a softly covering wing.

A sense of retreat, detachment, composure, inhabits the place. To be sheltered at God's side, to be covered by His hand, gives the soul a peculiar serenity. He breaks the arrows of the adversary and shatters his spear. During hostilities between nations, ships are commonly convoyed by cruisers, destroyers, aircraft, but a better escort is here provided: "He shall give his angels charge over thee"; they bring the guests of God safely upon their way. The hidden protections of God are with His people everywhere, and no terror can make them afraid.

There is comfort, courage, confidence in its secret. There is no sympathy so deep or so sufficient as the sympathy of God. He is swift to recognise and swift to reciprocate every affection; "Because he hath set his love upon Me therefore will I deliver him; I will be with him in trouble." It has been said that not many people have the aptitude that makes a successful visitor to a sick-room. "Spare me," says Matthew Arnold, "spare me the whispering, crowded room, the friends who come, and gape, and go." Few have the disposition, the essential quality, to be a friend in trouble, but that is where God excels. Communion with Him composes our fears, dries our tears, and sets us bravely on our feet girded and shod for the roughest road, or the last adventure.

THE PALM TREE

"The righteous shall flourish like the palm tree."

THE pictorial language of scripture is due to the imagination of Eastern peoples; "The righteous shall grow like the palm tree." The palm tree has a remarkable erectness, not often will you see a crooked palm tree; they generally stand upright as if they grew to illustrate some idea. "Mark the perfect man and behold the upright, for the end of that man is peace."

The palm tree has an attractive stateliness, a certain self-respecting dignity; it throws out its fronds on high, opening them wide to wind and sun, and yet forming a gentle screen for the protection of the fruit that grows around the base of the springing fronds. Stateliness of character never comes down to meanness and a lie.

The fruitfulness of the palm tree is a conspicuous part of its value; its produce yields food, drink, clothing and shelter. It is one of the most profitable of tropical trees. The Christian is known by the fruitfulness of his life. The fruitful tree is the joyful recompense of man's cultivation; the fruitful life is the gladness of God.

The palm tree is the common emblem of peace; it is the symbol of triumph and of victory. The final vision of the redeemed is of a great multitude which no man could number wearing white robes and having palms in their hands. The ultimate triumph is the victory of peace; the righteous shall carry the palm:

> Love shall tread out the baleful fires of anger,
> And in their ashes plant the palm of peace.

.   .   .   .   .

> God of our fathers, known of old,
>   Lord of the far-flung battle line,
> Beneath whose awful hand we hold
>   Dominion over palm and pine,—
> Lord God of Hosts, be with us yet,
>   Lest we forget—lest we forget.

A ROYAL PROCLAMATION

"The Lord reigneth."

THE proclamation of the king is the first pronouncement, "The Lord reigneth." The psalm marks the beginning of a group of psalms called the Royal or Accession Psalms; they celebrate the sovereignty of Jehovah; He assumes His government, and He appears clothed with majesty and with strength. His appearance has a royalty beyond any earthly comparison; all human monarchies bow before the King Eternal.

The permanence of His reign is announced. His throne is established of old and He is from everlasting. From uncounted years behind us to uncountable years before us, God's throne endures undimmed and unchanged, uncreated and undying; the age of the world is as nothing to Him, our minds are lost in His eternity, our arithmetic cannot reckon His years.

The power of His government is acknowledged. On the side of the Clifton Gateway at Niagara appear the words, "The floods, O Lord, have lifted up their voice and made a mighty noise." The flood of waters represents one of the most powerful forces known to the ancients. The Hebrew people knew how terrible and devastating floods of water can be, but their confidence was in the Lord; He is mightier than the noise of many waters or the mighty waves of the sea. The sea is man's untamed element; he can use its tides but he cannot control them. Only God is King of the sea, and He is monarch of the universe, exercising marvellous patience towards the warfare which man's sinfulness wages against His house and throne. The black floods of world wars do not surpass His power. "If you have a creed," said Carlyle, "you can afford to wait." God is not capricious or impulsive, He can afford to wait.

> God moves in a mysterious way
> His wonders to perform;
> He plants His footsteps in the sea
> And rides upon the storm.
>
> Blind unbelief is sure to err,
> And scan His work in vain;
> God is His own interpreter,
> And He will make it plain.

DIVINE OBSERVATION

"The Lord knoweth the thoughts of man."

THE complaint is made that wicked and unscrupulous men persuade themselves and boast before other people that "the Lord shall not see, neither shall the God of Jacob regard it". They encourage themselves in their wickedness, they think that God pays no attention to them, therefore they can do what they like without restraint. The wish is father to the thought; they do not want to be seen, they hope they are not seen, they make themselves believe that they are not seen, whereas the Psalmist is sure that nothing escapes the divine eye; God's acute observation misses nothing, and God's justice will not omit the penalties due alike to the open and the secret sins of mankind.

He is equally sure that God's insight is as searching as His oversight. "He that planted the ear, shall He not hear? He that formed the eye, shall He not see?" The great divine artificer who formed the amazing delicacy of the ear and fashioned the intricacies of the eye must Himself have hearing and sight beyond our range of sound and vision; our powers are often defective but His are perfect. "His eyes were as a flame of fire," said John, describing the vision of Patmos.

The singer is equally certain that the divine foresight is able to see things in the distance, even to see the end from the beginning. He is able to anticipate the events that are likely to befall, hence the confession, "When I think my foot is slipping, Thy goodness, O God, holds me up; when doubts crowd into my mind, Thy comfort cheers me." God's preventive grace averts many a stumble, and saves us from our own forebodings. He that gave us minds looking before and after is Himself as familiar with the distant as with the near, with the past and the future as with the present; nothing escapes Him.

WHO OWNS THE SEA?

"The sea is His, He made it."

THE creation of the sea was an act of God. "The sea is His, He made it." The ownership of the sea-fronts is claimed by neighbouring nations; fishing and trading are subject to many restrictions. The great powers attempt to dominate the adjacent oceans, and have sometimes called them by their names. The rights and titles of the sea have caused many disputes among nations, disputes that have even challenged the ownership of God.

The control of the sea is His, none else can tame its raging; no human power can put a bit in its teeth and a bridle on its neck. The tides of the sea are independent of men. King Canute had no power to stay the flow of its currents. "I came about like a well-handled ship," said the poet of an experience tantamount to a conversion, "there stood at the helm that Unknown Steersman we call God." The able handling of a ship requires great skill, but who can handle the sea? Christ alone had this authority; "What manner of man is this that even the wind and the waves obey him?" At the last He will make the sea give up its dead.

The chart of the sea is His, "Thy way is in the sea and thy path in the great waters." Road building has become a great science and all the roads that men have made may be easily lost, but no trail is so swiftly obliterated as the tracks of ships at sea. Not long do they leave a trace behind. There is only One who needs no human chart or compass, because His way is in the sea. No life that has accepted His guidance is ever lost in its going; He brings each life His own way home.

All this, says the singer, constrains the glad and grateful heart to worship. "O come let us sing unto the Lord, let us come before His presence with thanksgiving." Work is one side of life, the other side is worship; our business is to give each its due attention so as to preserve a balanced life.

III

THE ELEMENTS OF GOD'S SUPREMACY

"Honour and majesty, strength and beauty."

PART of the eternal sovereignty of God is the supremacy of goodness. He does not compel the obedience of mankind; He offers inducement and recompense for the encouragement of goodness. The superiority which Israel recognised in God as against the pagan gods was not only that He had greater power than they, but that His righteousness was greater, His will was constant and reliable; His compassion and patience were such as to make obedience attractive and goodness a supreme benefit.

The supremacy of His holiness sets Him above the moods and passions of pagan gods and pagan people. "Honour and majesty are before Him, strength and beauty are in His sanctuary." This revelation of God's character makes the full heart exclaim, "O worship the Lord in the beauty of holiness." Health is wholesomeness of body, holiness is wholesomeness of spirit. Encouragement is given to others, "Say among the heathen that the Lord reigneth." "He shall judge the people righteously." The reliability of His character makes Him for ever supreme; character in God and man is the chiefest of values.

The supremacy of gladness issues from the other supremacies. God did not make the earth for gloom or the eyes of His people for tears; He made the earth for gladness, "Let the field be joyful and the trees of the wood rejoice before the Lord." The heart of the singer is filled with ecstasy, his soul is set to merry music and he calls upon the heavens and the earth and the sea to join in the chorus of praise to God. The gospel came with song, revivals of religion are revivals of song; singing is the marching music of its ultimate supremacy.

WHAT YOU CAN DO TO GOD

" Ye that love the Lord, hate evil."

THE first question in the Shorter Catechism is, "What is man's chief end?" and the swift answer is, "Man's chief end is to glorify God and to enjoy Him for ever." This psalm is a simple exposition of the same truth. Here are some of the things God wants you to do.

You can trust Him. "Clouds and darkness are round about Him"; all things are not as clear as a summer day. Mystery and storm and earthquake perturbed the ancients as they perturb us, but the Psalmist confided in God. Faith is often difficult but unfaith is more difficult. Clouds and darkness are not the only envelopment of God, light is sown for the righteous, the heavens declare His glory. There is light enough, as Browning suggested, "for us in the dark to rise by".

You can love Him. You cannot love by order. "Thou shalt love the Lord thy God with all thy heart" is not meant to command love, but to regulate it; it shows how God wants to be loved, not with a divided heart but with the whole heart. The gifts inducing love in ancient times were of earth and home, of love and life; we have a better stimulus, "We love Him because He first loved us." The love of God must be safeguarded by wholesome antipathy to every wrong thing, "Ye that love Jehovah, hate evil." A good lover is a good hater; he hates badness from love of goodness.

You can rejoice in Him. Emphasis is laid upon gladness; it is not merely temperamental cheerfulness, or the buoyancy of vigorous health, it springs from the sense of the goodness of God. The harvest of sin is sorrow, but the fruit of the Spirit is joy. A pure perennial spring of gladness is in God, the flow never ceases, the music is never silent. God is King, that fact sets the heart at rest about all mystery; that fact should give our lives a gladness that will infect other people with hope.

A NEW SONG

"O sing unto the Lord a new song."

THE new song is the result of a new experience; "No day without its line" was the motto and purpose of the ancient poet. This meant not merely a disciplined and regulated output but the discovery of new things to write about, new events to celebrate, new emotions to express, new gratitudes, new petitions. Life was never stale, it was always turning up some new thing.

The new song is to have salvation for its theme. God is always doing some saving thing. When His judgments overthrow wrong, it is that He might preserve goodness from perishing; He is always on the side of the pure, that is the secret of its permanence. What He approves has the promise of life.

The new song is to be of judgment as well as of salvation. What He disapproves is under sentence of death. There is no righteous judgment in the earth, knowledge is too limited, too partial, too prejudiced. God alone sits free from prejudice; He alone knows all the hidden part, the part that cannot express itself, that cannot be lifted into consciousness; the unexpressed and inexpressible are an open book to Him.

The new song is for all the earth to sing. Your national anthems are narrow and discordant compared with this world anthem, this universal praise. You cannot afford to miss this new song, it is the prelude to the new song of paradise; all the earth is summoned to make a joyful noise to God.

The simple fact for the modern world is that nationalism has gone. There never was mere nationalism in great thinking, great art, great music. Above all other men the redeemed man is a citizen of the world because he is a citizen of the Kingdom of God whose songs are world anthems of redemption.

WHAT GOD CAN DO

"They called and He answered them."

"The Lord reigneth", this is the refrain of these royalist songs —songs that celebrate the divine monarchy. His reign is an active rule. Consider what He does:

He answers prayer. The saying is history, it is stated as a fact for men, "They called upon the Lord and He answered them." The statement is repeated as a fact for God, "Thou answeredst them, O Lord our God." When you speak to Him, He speaks back; He never lets a petition go unheard, He never permits a cry to agitate the atmosphere and then perish, a sound signifying nothing.

He forgives sin. "Thou wast a God that forgavest them." To forgive is God's greatest work, and for this men prostrate themselves in penitence, making confession and gratefully accepting pardon, accepting more than pardon, accepting forgiveness. A king can pardon a subject, a judge may pardon a criminal, but neither king nor judge can forgive. "Who can forgive sin but God only?" Forgiveness cancels out the wrong itself, obliterates the whole; God alone is capable of so great an act.

He executes judgment. "Thou tookest vengeance of their inventions." The great invention that provoked His displeasure was the making of the golden calf in the wilderness; their setting up of a substitute for God, making something which their hands formed, and calling it God to the accompaniment of pagan rites borrowed from pagan peoples. It was a miserable reversion to type. The worshippers of God must keep His testimonies and never turn aside to worship idols.

> The dearest idol I have known,
>   Whate'er that idol be,
> Help me to tear it from Thy throne,
>   And worship only Thee.

RIGHT IDEAS ABOUT GOD

"Know ye that the Lord He is God."

THE first essential to the ideal state is right ideas about God. This saying points the way to all future well-being. For the final truth about God we must refer to the teaching of Christ, but here is something to start with:

God is Universal. A trumpet-call is sounded forth to all the earth summoning all to worship God. He is the Maker of us all, the Creator of our life, and the Creator of what was good in Israel and in any country. Many things are restricted by climate, by condition, by constitution, by language, but religion is as universal as the life of man. All mankind are summoned to the sanctuary; there is no more an outer court of the Gentiles, there is one God and one sanctuary and one worship.

God is Absolute. All His attributes are on the same scale, because He made us He can make us again; that is the hope of our spoiled and broken human nature. His absoluteness is beneficent and saving. He is the Shepherd and we are His sheep; this was a familiar image to pastoral people, it revealed to them the care God exercises for His own, the patience He displays, the protection He supplies, the provision He makes.

God is Good. Not merely for a day while the mood serves but continually by principle, by character, and by nature, never deviating from His goodness for a moment. His mercy is everlasting, His truth endureth to all generations. Since God is good the first obligation of His people is to be good too; the worst penalty of our sin is separation from Him; the best advantage of forgiveness is communion with Him. Those who really come to Him go no more from Him.

CHANGING TUNE

"I will sing . . . I will behave myself."

THE tune accompanies a song, "I will sing of mercy and judgment." The singer exults in mercy because mercy is God's love in action; he exults in judgment because God will not falsely charge any man with wrong. His righteousness is not vindictive. There are vocations that make those who follow them suspicious of other people; they are always on the alert for a fault, they pounce on it like a cat on a thing of prey, they exaggerate it so as to appear skilful in its detection; but mercy saves from every fault, mercy gives a chance to the fallen to rise again.

The song changes to a prayer, "Unto thee, O Lord, will I sing." God is the source of all good, no song about goodness can omit the God who alone is good and from whom all goodness springs. There is no goodness without Him. "O when wilt Thou come unto me?" is the yearning of one who wants for himself the goodness of God; God's coming is his expectation and his hope, God's arrival will be his salvation.

The prayer formulates a vow; what begins with a song and changes to a prayer now becomes a covenant. The closer the man comes to God the more he wants to be like Him, and the more he resolves to seek that likeness. "I will behave myself wisely in a perfect way, I will set no wicked thing before mine eyes, I will not know a wicked person." His life, his home, his friends, his servants will be formed and chosen suitably to his covenant with God. To make all one's life, from innermost centre to outermost circumference, one consistent whole, one united piece to God the Father, is a condition worthy of the best endeavour.

MERCY AT WORK

" Thou shalt arise and have mercy upon Zion."

THE mercy of God is always opportune; that starts the song. When the heart was destitute and all life a dreary and desolate thing, the expectation survived that God would have mercy upon Zion. Things had come to such a pass that the spirit of the man felt intuitively that "the time to favour Zion, the set time was come". The emergency itself declared that the time was opportune, the season of necessity was the season of mercy. Our human contingencies invite the interpositions of God; at the end of our resources we discover the beginnings of God.

His mercy is effective. Mercy is not a sentiment, a doctrine, an abstract creed, it is one of the most effective forces, it is one of the energies of God. When He gets working His glory will appear; out of the ruins will arise a new shrine; out of the fractured clay that refused the potter's skill will come another vessel. Mercy casts nothing away, mercy finds a reason for hope where other eyes see no promise at all; good times will yet come to Zion and men will sing of her restoration.

His mercy is resolute. The fixed intention of God was to rebuild the temple and restore His worship in the reconstructed shrine. His praise would be renewed where the silence of neglect had reigned, He would re-assemble His people in the once deserted and forsaken shrine. The set time is come, is come now. The singer may not be there to see its arrival; man's life is brief and uncertain but God is for ever, therefore the future is bright with hope.

> Ye fearful saints fresh courage take,
> The clouds ye so much dread
> Are big with mercy, and shall break
> With blessings on your head.

DIVINE DIMENSIONS

" Plenteous in mercy."

THE scale of God's forgiveness is clearly stated, "He forgiveth all thine iniquities", all of them; to make the fact more real to his own spirit the forgiven man says that his sin is taken away, removed as far as East is from the West, a safe distance; it is blotted out so that no record remains; it is cast into the depths of the sea beyond all recovery. This effective treatment affects not some sins but the whole brood of evil.

The measure of His kindness is beyond our calculation; His kindness is heavens high and worlds wide; that is its measurement in terms of space; in terms of charity, He heals our sicknesses and crowns us with loving-kindness; in terms of life, He renews our youth like the eagle's; in terms of sympathy, He is better than the best of fathers to their children. Language sinks exhausted in its attempt to express His kindness.

The extent of His goodness. Man's life is frail and quickly over, he perishes like grass, he withers like a flower, but God's mercy runs exhaustless through all generations. He observes such as keep His covenant, but above all our merit His mercy endures, "Bless the Lord, O my soul." But you must charge your memory to keep these benefits in mind. Don't forget them, their remembrance is a spur to better devotion. Such as keep His covenant and remember His commandments to do them, these faithful and practically minded people inherit the promises. God and man expect you and me to be about our Father's business, the sober, serious business of getting the Will of God done upon the earth and in our lifetime; you and I will have no other time.

GOD OVER ALL

"O Lord my God, Thou art very great."

GOD'S universal superintendence is here under review. He covers Himself with light as with a garment, clothes Himself with majesty, makes the clouds His chariots and the winds His wings, sets the bounds of the sea and so overspreads the world with His power that nothing walks with aimless feet. We confess that God moves in a mysterious way, but if the process is often puzzling the end is sure, for all things are under control, all things are subject to direction. His superintendence will effect the final good, plucking advantage even from adversity.

His providence is as widespread as His rule. He contrives to make all things serve a beneficent purpose, His rain is in the heavens and His springs in the valleys to provide drink for every thirsty desire, to make grass to grow for cattle, and herb for the service of man. His providence is on the essential scale, the harvests of the earth and the supplies of the sea are sufficient for the needs of all living things. If any hunger it is because of man's faulty distribution of the benefits of earth and sea.

We confess universal dependence. "These wait all upon Thee —that Thou givest them they gather." His open hand fills them, His closed hand is a trouble to them; it is upon His bounty all things rely, and for this every sincere heart feels its own gratitude. St. Francis observed that after drinking, the birds lifted up their little beaks as if to say "Thank you", for all God's benefits. Shall we be surpassed in courtesy by the sparrow?

INSTRUMENT OF REDEMPTION

"He sent a man before them."

GOD's instrument must always be suitable to His hand and consistent with His work—"He sent a man before them." When commissions ripen He seeks the man who will serve the occasion. For human ends He uses human instruments; at every stage of progress He sent a man, Abraham, Joseph, Moses. The worst wrongs that men suffer are done by men; correspondingly the best blessings that men enjoy are by God's direction the gifts of man to man. Man is the instrument of this world's good or ill.

The crowning instrument of man's redemption was Son of Man and Son of God, Jesus Christ. God spake in time past unto the fathers by the prophets, but in the latter days He spoke to men by His Son.

O loving wisdom of our God! When all was sin and shame,
A second Adam to the fight, And to the rescue came.

O, wisest love! that flesh and blood, Which did in Adam fail,
Should strive afresh against the foe, Should strive and should
   prevail.

He sent a Man! The saying of Jeremy Taylor comes to mind: "When God would save man, He did it by way of a Man!" The Man Christ Jesus had a commission all His own (John ix. 4). There needs no second Man, no second Name, no second Cross.

The human instrument continues to be God's quest. Jesus perpetuates God's method; "As the Father hath sent Me, even so send I you." The redemption of the world goes forward by contacts of life with life. The redeemed life goes on redeeming others; the real missing link by which the lost are lost is the absence of the saving instrument, "I have no man when the water is troubled to bring me to the pool." "How can I understand," asked the puzzled Ethiopian, "except some man teach me?" Tennyson uttered a cry for the essential man, "Ah, God, for a man . . . one still strong man in a blatant land!" It is more than a poet's quest, it is God's quest, "Whom shall I send, and who will go for us?" Witness David Brainerd's aspiring reply, "Oh! that I might be a flaming fire in the service of my God. Here I am; Lord, send me; send me to the end of the earth; send me to the rough, the savage pagans of the wilderness."

RIGHTEOUSNESS IN SEASON

" At all times."

IF ever you are disposed to ask whether one can always do right, here is a sufficient answer: "Blessed is he that doeth righteousness at all times." We all fail and sometimes badly fail, but there was One who never made a slip, who was able to say, "I do always those things that please Him." Most of us do the right sometimes, but not at all times; we have our slips and our mistakes and our defeats, but He did righteousness at all times.

We do most things fitfully, we chop and change our conduct and our plans, we are here to-day and there to-morrow; we weary of righteousness and resign from it for a season. It is not easy to pick out of history the men who formed their lives to one certain and constant course. But Christ stands where the rest of us fail, His righteousness was always in season. He never broke away on any excursion of His own, never took a line independent of the Father's will.

Here then is a higher law than that which custom has established; it is above what is popular, it transcends what is profitable, it supersedes what is merely pleasant, it surpasses what is clever; the final test of speech and action is this, "Is it right?" That is Christ's high law: if it is right, do it, only that; do it, win or lose; do it, sink or swim; he cannot lose who sides with God.

> For right is right since God is God,
> And right the day must win;
> To doubt would be disloyalty,
> To falter would be sin.

BOOK 5

Psalms 107–150

Equally with anything that has been said as common to the Psalms, there remains the mention of Worship, the assembly of the people in Tabernacle and Temple to worship God.

To worship God is the resolute purpose of one who has to act alone: "As for me, I will come into Thy house" (Ps. v. 20). Another reflects that worship requires some readjustment of life (Ps. xv. 24). Another puts on record the tension and trouble that he endured "Until I went into the sanctuary of God, then I understood" (Ps. lxxiii, 6). Another rejoices that he was invited to share the good thing: "I was glad when they said unto me, Let us go into the house of the Lord" (Ps. cxxii. 1). The Hebrew Psalm was the preface to the Christian Hymn.

But the instinct to worship has wider bounds. So strong is the constraint of human intuition and the sense of dependence that the forms of worship were preserved even when the object of worship was unknown. The apostle Paul found at Athens an altar "To The Unknown God"; a significant creation and a significant confession. Near the Roman Forum I halted beside an altar with the inscription, "To God or Goddess whichever it be". There I felt the touch of human nature that makes the whole world kin. Worship is an intuition within the breast. At its lowest level it may be fear. But Christian worship is the answer of the human spirit to the love of God as revealed in Jesus Christ.

REDEMPTION IN EXTREMITY

"Then they cried unto the Lord in their trouble, and He saved them out of their distresses."

OUR human extremities are reached when our own resources are exhausted and there is nothing more that we can do; if anything is to be done, it must be done by someone with greater power than human skill.

The people were oppressed and scattered in all directions, they wandered in the wilderness hungry and thirsty and homeless, with no landmarks to bring them upon their way nor any knowledge of the direction they should take. The need started a cry and God sent swift guidance. Four times in the psalm is the cry raised and four times is it answered. God's deliverances keep pace with our distresses.

The extremity that afflicts men may take the form of sickness and sorrow; darkness and discontent may be a wasting trial; humiliated and broken down they cry to God, and He sends immediate relief. The cry of trouble may come from those who feel that they have brought their troubles upon themselves; their afflictions are the result of their own transgressions, but they find as these people found, that even from the depth of darkness God can make light to arise.

The cry of the storm-tossed rises above the sound of the tempest, the souls of the mariners melted because of fear, but in answer to their petition God proved Himself the Captain of the sea. "He bringeth them to the haven where they would be." This verse is inscribed in the memorial to Sir John Franklin and his companions, which was erected in 1858, near the spot where the exploring party spent their first winter in the Arctics. Always there is survival out of trouble: "These are they that came out of great tribulation"; they did not go under, they were not lost, they recovered from every extremity. You will not sink and you will not break, God will see to it.

IN QUEST OF LEADERS

"Who will lead me into Edom?"

THE question "Who will lead me?" is repeated because it is important. The first part of this psalm is repeated from Psalm 57, and the second part from Psalm 64; repetition is not a mistake, it is a form of emphasis. Some things have to be said a second time because at the first saying the listener was not paying attention, he failed to realise what was being said or what was meant, and therefore the thing had to be said again.

The question is repeated because it has not yet been answered, "Who will lead me into Edom?" no volunteer had yet come forward. There are difficult enterprises and unpopular causes that wait for leadership and support. "If you would be famous," said a great leader to a friend, "go and join yourself to some unpopular cause and help it forward to wholesome victory." Edom may be the citadel of some entrenched evil, like the liquor trade in England, or a vicious habit like gambling, the dark fortress of sensuality, the towering castle of pride, the gloomy stronghold of stubbornness and apathy, the dark abode of lust, or several of these together.

The question awaits an answer now, "Who will bring me into the strong city?" There are multitudes not yet captured for Christ, lands not yet won, the world's press, public opinion, war, selfishness, disease, irreligion, the new paganism, all these are citadels to be won. You have come to the kingdom for such a time as this. God will lead us into Edom, but He is waiting for the volunteer.

The singer himself is a pattern of purpose, "O God, my heart is fixed." He is no mournful and protesting conscript. His heart is in the business cheerfully, for his heart is fixed on God and what God will do. By His help the people will do valiantly: Edom will be taken, the strong city will be captured. There is no citadel of evil that cannot be stormed; stay your heart on God and tackle it.

THE FATE OF A NAME

"Let their name be blotted out."

SOME names have been deleted from family or church roll because they became an undesirable possession. "Let their name be blotted out," urges the Psalmist concerning those who had sorely persecuted him. It is a sorrowful thing to remove a name from any association of virtue and goodness. There is in the memoirs of Thomas Boston a blank line. A name has been kept from publication, its wearer was an adversary stirred up by Satan. The minister of Ettrick in forwarding the name of the delinquent added, "But let it remain blank for ever." The name is still blank after more than two hundred years. Browning makes final the fate of the lost leader: "Blot out his name then, record one lost soul more; let him never come back to us: never glad confident morning again."

Some names have been restored after deletion; there are records of prodigal sons and prodigal daughters whose names were deleted from the family Bible; but, after they had exhausted the indulgence they coveted, they came back and their names were re-inscribed in the family book as Old Mortality re-inscribed, upon the worn and wasted stones, the names of the martyrs that he was unwilling to leave to time's oblivion.

Some names have been honourably preserved from their first writing, they have remained faithful to their vow, no reproach ever threatened their removal. The book of life is the family volume of the household of God; there our names are in surest keeping, safe from the tampering fingers of men.

> Is your name written there,
> On the page white and fair,
> In the book of the kingdom,
> Is your name written there?

WAYSIDE STREAMS

"He shall drink of the brook in the way."

IN the heat and weariness of conflict the king came upon a wayside stream, and the brook flooded his inner life with new energy and fighting power. The King here is the coming Messiah who accepts the limitations which we share.

The necessity of the wayside streams arises from our human limitations. We easily reach the limit of our powers, we quickly exhaust our resources. A day is as much as we can stand of anything, the end of the day finds us tired; night comes on with its gift of rest, we drink of the brook of sleep and are refreshed.

The accessibility of the wayside streams matches their necessity. Too often we think that the things we want are in the ends of the earth, and we can only get them after long waiting or by distant travel, but some of the best things are close at hand. The Scriptures are a river of refreshment to the devout reader; the Lord's Day is a brook by the way, its waters refresh the soul; the bells of the sanctuary ring out the summons to worship, "Ho every one that thirsteth, come ye to the waters." Friendship, prayer, solitude, good books may be wayside streams to you.

The vitality communicated makes the experience eminently desirable, "therefore shall he lift up the head". The drooping spirit is exalted, the tired nature is renewed in its energy and purpose. In his tale *With the Russian Pilgrims to Jerusalem*, the author says that "a priest delicately forewarned the pilgrims going down to the muddy little Jordan river—'Do not expect anything like the Volga or the Dvina or the Dnieper. The Jordan is not grand. Much in the Holy Land wears an ordinary appearance!'" Many of the blessings of our lives are as incidental and ordinary as wayside flowers and wayside streams, but without them our very souls would warp and wither.

FORGET-ME-NOTS

"To be remembered."

THIS simple, single-hearted man has looked on the works of God in the world: they have filled his heart with wonder and inspired his pen. He sees that God's works are designed for the good of God's people; beauty and utility unite. The psalm combines with the next in forming an introduction to the psalms sung at the Passover, hence its memorial character.

The memorial day. "He hath made his wonderful works to be remembered." The first divine memorial was the Sabbath. It celebrated the completion of God's creative plan; it was His rest day and He shared it as such with mankind, "Remember the Sabbath day to keep it holy." The day was to be separate in character and use from the six days of labour, it was to be sanctified to men in rest, and hallowed to God in worship.

The memorial rite. God's people were kept in long servitude. Because their labour was indispensable, and was part of the potential wealth of the country, the Egyptians resisted every attempt at emancipation until God adopted extreme measures in the death of the first-born of every Egyptian household; the resistance of Pharaoh was broken, the Passover became the memorial to Israel of the preservation of its households.

The memorial book. God gave His commandments as a guide to conduct and life, a writing to keep His people in remembrance of His providence. The book of the law was not to depart out of their mouth, but to be the subject of remembrance and meditation and action: "A good understanding have all they that do His commandments." Obedience is the gateway to knowledge; every reverent act is an advance into light.

HEART CONDITIONS

"His heart is fixed."

THE blessings that attend the upright man are spread over all his life, his home and his possessions. The heart of this psalm is the heart of the man.

There are more heart troubles in the world to-day than ever before. The pace and pressure of modern life, the anxiety about business, the uncertainty of employment, the insecurity of peace fill one with foreboding. "Alas, how I leave my country," sighed a dying statesman. Disquiet haunts the mind like an evil spirit, anxiety sucks the life-blood of multitudes, they carry the burden of a troubled heart.

Some people seem to live above fear; they do not yield to agitation, they are not moved and disturbed by passing events, they see further and are quiet, they strike deeper roots and are sure, they hold or are held by some immovable object, they are not afraid of evil tidings, they are not disturbed by wild rumours, their life is fixed in God, they own the tranquil heart. "Blessed is the man that feareth the Lord, he shall not be moved, he shall not be afraid, his heart is fixed."

That is the secret of tranquillity: "His heart is established." There are countless numbers who would purchase tranquillity if it were offered for sale; if some far land held its secret they would go on pilgrimage to find it; but it is not for purchase, it is not for sale; no treasure island holds this precious thing and yet it can be had without money and without price. "His heart is fixed, trusting in the Lord," that does it. "Let not your heart be troubled, believe in God"; the trusting heart is the tranquil heart.

> And Thou, O Lord, by Whom are seen
> Thy creatures as they be,
> Forgive me if too close I lean
> My human heart on Thee.

But you cannot lean too close; it is that very closeness that covers all risks, settles all questions, and banishes all fears.

WHO IS LIKE HIM?

"Who is like unto the Lord?"

THIS is the first of six hymns of praise which were sung at Jewish festivals, particularly at the Passover. It begins with a joyful outburst of praise to God.

His praise is perpetual, "from this time forth and for evermore". The events of history start the song. Because of what God is and what He has done the praise begins; but history and experience are not a closed book, every day adds to the knowledge and experience of His grace, and so His praise is renewed daily from the rising to the setting sun. The song is never stale because life is never stale; each new experience starts some new song.

His grace is universal. "The Lord is high above all nations and His glory above the heavens." He swings earth and sky within their orbit, He sees things that are above and beneath, He is the besetting God from Whom there is no escape. No flight, be it ever so swift or far, can take the soul beyond His sight or care. When the impulse to escape takes hold of you, do not try to run from Him, run to Him.

His redemption is personal. God's providence is not active only over wide areas of life, doing big spectacular things. Man is spectacular, he loves show and self-advertisement, withholding his interest from little things, but God chooses the insignificant and makes them great. He sets the poor among princes; He rescues a child and makes him Moses; He redeems a slave and fashions him to a Joseph. The potter shapes one vessel at a time. The divine Potter lays His fingers around each life by itself to shape and use.

DOUBLE EVENTS

" When Israel went out . . . the house of Jacob."

THIS psalm is jubilant in acknowledgment and honour of what God did for Israel in the wilderness.

Notice the double name. "Israel" and "Jacob" are the two names by which the people became known. Jacob meant the family group, the family tradition, the family weakness, the transmission of the faulty frailty of the father. Israel became the title of the nation, the princeliness to which Jacob rose and at which the people were to aim. "Jacob" meant the abandoned past, "Israel" meant the coveted future, weakness changed to strength, the crooked was made straight.

Mark the double deliverance. Twice the children of Israel had to cross the waterways of the world; at their going out of Egypt the sea fled before the power of God and made a way for them. The second took place at Jordan when the people were held up by the river barrier. Yesterday God made a passage through the sea, to-day He will make a path across the river. Nothing baffles Him; nothing finally frustrates Him.

Record the double gift. Twice the people's thirst was quenched by waters from the rock. The first new spring was at Horeb where He gave them water from the flint; nearly forty years later the rocks at Kadesh gave a second stream. One gift does not exhaust the resources of grace, each new need finds a new supply. It is not a new religion that the world needs, but some fresh discovery of the abundance of the old.

SMALL AND GREAT

" He will bless both small and great."

GOD's effective mercy is the subject of praise. The test that is applied to most things is the test of effectiveness—"Does it work?" The psalm elaborates the ineffectiveness of the idols that the pagans worship; the writer contrasts their helplessness with the effective activities of God. They are the work of man's hands but Jehovah made the heavens; they are idols that men have fashioned, they have ears but they hear not, mouths but they cannot speak, eyes that cannot see, hands that are useless, feet that cannot walk. To make them the object of veneration is folly, to trust them for any benefit is wasted confidence: the one object of worship is God, the one assurance for living is to trust Him.

God's inclusive mercy is a further subject of praise, "He will bless both small and great." It is a comfort that God takes notice of the small, our earthly distinctions have no recognition with Him; our last is often His first, and our first is His last. His order is final and absolute; He alone knows all, passes none over, makes no mistake. "I saw the dead, small and great, stand before God." It was a vision of the inclusiveness of mercy; and even if it might be the inclusiveness of judgment it shows that God leaves none out. "Satan will not get one lamb out of the flock of Christ unmissed," wrote Alexander Peden to the Covenanters imprisoned on the Bass Rock. Every life has an inherent value of its own, but that value is enhanced beyond computation by the fact that Christ died for that life; His passion re-values the lives of men, women and little children; you must see them through Christ's eyes if you are to appreciate their real worth.

"BECAUSE"

"Because He hath inclined His ear unto me."

IT is good to find reasons for things: reasons that explain actions and feelings: reasons that warrant faith and hope: reasons that justify the purpose we cherish.

Here is good reason for gratitude: "I will love the Lord because He hath heard my voice and my supplications." The goodness of God was the inspiration of affection; he does not hesitate to say that he loves the Lord, his love springs out of gratitude; it is a spontaneous affection that rises out of the comfort received in sickness and in trouble: "I was brought low and He helped me," and from that experience of helpfulness the man's heart was open to his God.

A reason for prayer is given: "Because He hath inclined His ear unto me, therefore will I call upon Him as long as I live." When trouble and sorrow overtook him he called upon God and God answered. You never speak to Him but He speaks back. There is in Him no sullen mood of silence, He cherishes no grudge that makes Him refuse to speak; every prayer is heard and every prayer gets some reply.

An encouragement to devotion. When the hour of trial is past this man asks, "What shall I render unto the Lord?" God answers our cry, what answer have we to His beseechings and benefits? The answer that the soul gives for itself and to itself is, "Return unto thy rest, O my soul, for the Lord hath dealt bountifully with thee." He is not content to say this once, He says it twice and with full intention to do it. "Never lie in your prayers," says Jeremy Taylor; "never confess more than you really believe; never promise more than you mean to perform." But remember that His grace will never be lacking to your endeavour.

ACKNOWLEDGMENTS

" For His merciful kindness is great."

THE shortest of all the psalms! But it speaks to all people of the mercy of God and the eternity of His truth.

The range of God's mercy reveals His far-spreading purpose; all nations are included in it, all people are united within its scope. God's grace is universal, no barrier can shut it out, no wide-spreading sea can separate a soul from the reach of it. His heart is not subject to the separating prejudices that divide the human race, nation from nation and colour from colour; our petty divisions are limited to the earth, heaven overspreads all mankind with one pity and one affection. God is equal to the larger hope:

> Ye fearful saints, fresh courage take;
> The clouds ye so much dread
> Are big with mercy, and shall break
> In blessings on your head.

The extent of His favour is indicated. "His merciful loving-kindness is great toward us." It is the sentence of one whose words are few, not because he has little to say but because words are utterly inadequate to express the things he wants to say. God's kindness is not miserly, measuring His grace to us drop by drop; His kindness is generous, giving to us mercy that fills life to the brim, even to the overflow. John Milton incites the praise of the divine kindness:

> Let us, with a gladsome mind,
> Praise the Lord for He is kind:
> For His mercies aye endure,
> Ever faithful, ever sure.

The eternity of His truth is celebrated; it endureth for ever. There is no equivocation with Him, no hesitancy, no half-truths, no time-serving, no opportunism, waiting to see how the wind will blow or how the popular vote of men may incline. His truth is true for all time and for the endless ages after time. It is the one reliable thing in this inconstant world.

> For why? the Lord our God is good
> His mercy is for ever sure:
> His truth at all times firmly stood
> And shall from age to age endure.

IT IS BETTER

" It is better to trust in the Lord."

OF all the earthly creatures God has made, man is the greatest, he is the crown of creation. With capacity to rise, he can be a very angel in virtue; but that same capacity when perverted can make him very base. The Psalmist recognised the uncertain quality of human nature; you cannot depend on man, he can let you down very badly—"I think nothing of the world and the public," wrote Sir Ernest Shackleton from South Georgia. "They cheer you one minute and howl you down the next." Human favour and goodwill are fluctuating qualities. "It is better to trust in the Lord than to put confidence in man."

Princes of the royal house are educated in wisdom and in knowledge, they sit in the seat of power, they make laws, but they often fail in honour. The king of Italy and the king of Bohemia promised John Huss safe transport and safe custody; but they broke their promise; Huss was martyred. Thomas Wentworth carried a document signed by King Charles I which said, "Upon the word of a king, you shall not suffer in life, honour or fortune." But shortly afterwards his death-warrant was signed by the same monarch. "Put not your trust in princes," was his bitter last word. "It is better to trust in the Lord than to put confidence in princes."

The master builders disallowed a stone which afterwards proved indispensable to the structure they were making. Our Lord was rejected by the leaders of Israel, but He established a new Israel. The wisdom of this world comes to nought; it is better to trust in the Lord than to put confidence in experts! Concerning life and all it holds of merit or demerit, the last word is with God; that is a note of warning to some, it is a word of consolation for others. When John Foster was dying he was heard to repeat the words, "Trust in Christ—Trust in Christ." It is a great way to live and a great way to die.

LAMP-LIGHT

" Thy word is a lamp unto my feet and a light unto my path."

THERE are providences that are personal and private, "Thy word is a lamp"—a lantern to guide one's steps through the dark; not a sun or star for everybody but a lamp for you, limited to your immediate requirements : a hand-lamp in the room where you live, on the road you tread. In Christ's story of the ten virgins each had her own lamp; that must be part of your equipment for life.

There are providences that are public, as public as sun and moon and star; providences that we share with all the world, each of us can have all we want without depriving any other of all that he wants or claims.

> The sun whose beams most glorious are,
> Disdaineth no beholder.

The sunshine goes straight to the eye of every beholder and floods the world with light; so is the love of God, so is the grace of Christ. There is enough for each, enough for all, enough for evermore. Those who come first will not prejudice the chance of those who come after; there will be as much for the last as for the first.

The providences of God are progressive, from lamplight to sunlight, from a lighted candle in the dark to the lighted sun in the day; God leads from less to more, from good to better, from the providence of childhood to the providence of manhood, from the providence of earth to the providence of heaven. If the strain increases, if sorrows multiply, if temptations thicken, His grace will grow with every strain and match each hour.

Ruskin, writing of the portions of the Bible which he had been made to learn in boyhood, mentions, "That which cost me most to learn, and which was to my child's view, chiefly repulsive—the 119th Psalm—has now become of all the most precious to me."

The Psalm is arranged in stanzas, the eight lines of each stanza beginning with the Hebrew letter whose name appears at its head. There are twenty-two letters in the Hebrew alphabet and the Psalm conforms to that number of stanzas.

Additional space has been given to this Psalm and in the following pages two stanzas have been taken together under the simple title of some representative word or phrase.

THE PRECIOUSNESS OF GOD'S LAW

Wholeness   *Psalm 119: 1–16*

THERE are repeated references in this long psalm to the value of things that are done with the whole heart. Twice over, *seeking* with the whole heart is the subject of reference (v. 2, v. 10); half-hearted searching never merited the full joy of discovery. Twice over is the *keeping of the law* with the whole heart the subject mentioned (v. 34, v. 69). Twice over does he refer to *praying with the whole heart* (v. 59, v. 145). True devotion is of this essential quality. It is good to be a whole man in all we do. We read of "half believers" and "half men"; men of divided loyalties.

God is no friend of the life that is parcelled out among a variety of interests, spread over a wide field of many attachments in which He only counts as one, and gets a small portion like the rest. He wants the wholly devoted life. Give Him all there is of you; no half measures, no broken pieces, no reservations, no keeping back part of the gift, and no pretending that the part is the whole.

There is an impressive unity and simplicity about the life that undistractedly loves and serves God with the whole heart. Such a life will not be easily seduced from its first love.

A Trinity of Desire   *Psalm 119: 17–32*

Here is a man who knows what he wants. Three things he asks for. His first petition is for *opened eyes* that he might behold wondrous things out of God's law (v. 18). You know the saying that every common bush is afire with God but only he who sees takes off his shoes. It is so easy to miss treasures of beauty and of truth; "something lives in every hue Christless eyes have never seen". The Bible, says Bunyan, was very precious to me in those days, I began to look into it with new eyes, and read as I never did before.

His second petition was for an *instructed mind* (v. 27) that he might understand God's precepts. For us Christ is the great Interpreter of the Scriptures, the world's best Teacher. He makes the Bible live and speak. Bunyan continues: I was then never out of the Bible, either by reading or by meditation. It was as if it talked to me.

His third petition was for an *enlarged heart* (v. 32). You cannot add a cubit to your stature but that is of little account if you can grow a bigger heart. Learn to think and love beyond yourself. It is pathetic to meet people who are interested in a ruined cathedral but have no eye for a ruined life. There is a famine of generous hearts.

Twice over the writer of the psalm refers to his inclinations. The first mention is in a prayer that God will take charge of his inclinations; and in the second reference he seems to have forgotten that he had asked God to undertake the direction of his inclination for he says he did it himself (v. 112). The truth is that they did it together, God supporting every endeavour and helping to final victory. It is not often that a man confronts his inclinations, holds them at arms' length and challenges their right to rule his life.

Most of us, without doubt or question, obey our inclinations. We have a natural tendency in certain directions. There are preferences that assert themselves when any choice has to be made, and we choose the things we incline to. Our likes and dislikes rule our pleasures and our behaviour. The choice is not always between good and evil, it is often a choice between two things that may be equally good, between books and friends and opportunities, and it is then that our inclinations and disinclinations reveal themselves. They cannot be cancelled out, but they can be so directed by God that they become the wise guides of our way of life.

Comfort   *Psalm 119: 49–64*

Comfort is one of the attractive words in our tongue. Its meaning overspreads many of our necessities. Solace in sorrow is its first content, but it also means encouragement, cheer, the revival of hope, the recovery of desire, the lifting up of fallen purposes and intentions, the getting on one's feet again with brave and patient resolve after some disturbing experience.

The sad and the discouraged are a great multitude no man can number. The psalmist mentions *the comfort of hope* (vv. 49, 50). One of the great names given to God is "the God of Hope". He has hope of us and of our world when every hope of our own has perished. He continues to give the world little children assuredly hoping that each new generation will be better than the one before. And in Him hope persists through countless disappointments. Light your flickering torch at His flame. The *comfort of memory* is mentioned in verses 52 and 55. Hid in the mercies of our yesterdays are the promises of our tomorrows. Human love may suddenly come to an end but the love of God is for ever and ever. *The comfort of friends* and friendships (v. 63) is a great possession. Be friendly and you need never be lonely.

Discipline Psalm *119: 65–80*

We are not very old before we learn some of the disciplines that are common to human experience. We do not get all we want, we have to practise the art of doing without. We may feel ourselves entitled to certain possessions, privileges and pleasures but they do not come. And some contrary things that we would never seek are thrust upon us. This man makes the confession that discipline was good for him (v. 67). It corrected his way of life. It was a stern teacher but he profited by its influence.

I read the other day of one of God's suffering men that on his back he is worth half a dozen of some men on their feet! The psalmist enlarges upon his first experience of trial by this positive word: "It is good for me that I have been afflicted" (v. 71). Who of us has reached the triumphant endurance that says, "We glory in tribulation"? But the glory was in the outcome of the trial; in what affliction was actually producing of patience, experience, hope.

Again he accepts affliction as necessary for the development of his spirit (v. 75). God is faithful, He is not careless of our peace. He desires our good and permits only those things that will promote it.

Almost Psalm *119: 81–96*

There are some good things and some bad things that never happened, but they almost happened. That is the point in this confession of a life that had some precarious experiences. "They had almost consumed me," he says concerning his persecutors (v. 87). Think of the bad things that almost happened. "Almost consumed", but he survived, he got through, but it was touch and go; yet they did not make a complete end.

At another time, "My steps had almost gone"—he was as one pulled back from the edge of disaster, a brand plucked out of the fire. It was a narrow escape from failure and from shame. None of us can tell how often that has happened in our experience. At the last moment some intervention of God saved us from a crash in the region of faith and character.

Think of the good things that just missed history: "Almost thou persuadest me to be a Christian." Almost, but not quite! The little more and how much it is, the little less and what worlds away! It is alarmingly possible to be near to the Kingdom of God and yet miss it, to be within touching distance of some great experience, or some glad event, and yet lose it.

The Bible is the light of day and the lamp of night. Its flame lights every hour and circumstance of life. The poet Coleridge said that memory lights a lamp at the stern of the ship, shedding light upon the past but leaving the future as dark as ever. The sun is the master light of the material universe, the Bible is the master light of literature and of life. It lights the lamp of memory, bringing within our knowledge the names and events of long ages of history, and constantly charges us to keep in remembrance the many works and words of God in the past.

It lights the lamp of hope for the future, throwing forward its predictions and promises of what God will perform in the ages to come. Through the darkness of a confused and chaotic world shines the foregleam of the coming glory of Jesus Christ.

It lights the lamp of knowledge and assurance enabling us to share with the apostle the confidence that quietly asserts, "I know whom I have believed."

It lights the lamp of joy. Our Lord's repeated "Be of good cheer" sends us radiantly on our way with a song for the journey.

It lights the lamp of prayer; it is the first and best textbook of communion with God, our link with the unseen world.

Where Duty Calls   *Psalm 119: 113–128*

"Safety first" is not the slogan of the brave and the strong. Their watchword is "Duty first". Where duty calls or danger, the faithful must stand his ground. That is illustrated in the picture of the Roman sentry at the gates of Pompeii. When Mount Vesuvius erupted the overflow of the crater covered the city, the people fled, but the Roman sentry could not escape. Honour kept him where he was, and he perished where he stood.

The safety the psalmist seeks is not the safety of escape. In his prayer, "Hold Thou me up and I shall be safe", he asks for divine support. He asks that God will take his side against vain thoughts (vv. 113, 114), foolish action and selfish ambition. Our acts and habits begin in the mind. Let your secret thoughts be fair, they have far-reaching influences.

His safety also rests upon God's direction of his life, therefore he asks for God's strong hold upon his will and way. He asks further for God's intervention, "It is time for Thee to work" (v. 126). The feeling was mounting in his soul that unless God acted promptly the situation might pass beyond repair. The times and seasons of our lives, and of the world itself are in safest keeping. There is no room for fear.

Acquaint yourself with good books, those constant friends that never tire, teachers that never chide. This man has made friends of the testimonies of the Lord. They give him unbounded pleasure. He calls them wonderful (v. 129); they are the light of his eyes, the longing of his heart, the law of his life. Here in the word of God he finds the green pastures and the still waters; the lines are fallen unto him in pleasant places.

And after the pleasure they yield, he rejoices in their purity (v. 140). If you would be pure keep company with pure things. Here is *making pure*: "Wherewithal shall a young man cleanse his way? By taking heed unto Thy word." And here is *keeping pure*: "Thy word have I hid in my heart that I might not sin against Thee." To keep your garments white in a tainted world, to preserve an undefiled heart in a corrupt age is something no man can do except God be with him.

The next thing is the sense of permanence he finds in God's book; His testimonies are everlasting (v. 144). They are not subject to change, they need no revision, they have never been revoked. "Heaven and earth shall pass away," said Christ, "but my word shall never pass away." Cultivate the everlasting, and you too will be everlasting. Amid the swift flux of human things here is something stable and constant.

Stimulated   *Psalm 119: 145–160*

Three times in these verses the writer offers the prayer, "Quicken me according to Thy word". It is a prayer for larger, fuller life. When it is said that "He shall judge the quick and the dead" it is clear that the quick are those that are alive. To ask to be quickened implies that the man's life has gone flat and stale and unprofitable. The whole pace of things has gone slow and stodgy, dull and uninteresting. The thrill has gone out of living, the song has been silenced. Has it been the result of sickness, or of age; has some disappointing or discouraging experience flattened all his hopes, has some sorrow robbed him of his hope and keenness?

Whatever it is that has made his life poor and thin and half-hearted, whatever it is that has punctured our spirit and made us run on flat tyres, whatever it is that dooms a man to a dispirited existence, the one thing to do, the one way of recovery is to ask God to take the matter in hand. The whole purpose of Christ is to give life abundantly; no half measures here, but a brimful and bankful life, radiant in spirit, brave in its stride and victorious in hope.

It is a great thing to meet a happy man or woman. One of our poets has said that he would rather meet a happy man or woman than find a five pound note! Happiness has a value beyond financial computation.

Success is one of the secrets of happiness: "I rejoice at Thy word as one that findeth great spoil" (v. 162). He is a huntsman who brings his booty home, a warrior who comes with the recompense of battle on his shoulders, a merchant who returns with his gains from far markets.

What are the spoils of which this man boasts? Great peace is part of his spoil, and what a treasure that is. If men could buy it with money, they would sell all they possess to purchase it. Great happiness, great contentment is his; seven times a day he offers praise so full is he of song.

The treasures of God are sweeter than honey (v. 103), more precious than gold (v. 127) to him. He is as embarrassed as the apostle Paul to find the perfect word, the language adequate to his experience of God's mercy and truth and faithfulness. Gather your spoil, my friend. All treasures are hid in Christ and are available for His people; proffer your petition, put in your claim.

THE DECEITFUL TONGUE

"Lying lips and a deceitful tongue."

THE petition that breaks forth from a heart in distress is, "Deliver my soul, O Lord, from lying lips and from a deceitful tongue."

The deceitful tongue is the sorrow of God. He remonstrated with Israel because the people drew near to Him with their lips but their heart was far from Him; their worship was a mere pretence, a thing of words and nothing more. The tragic king knew how futile worship is when it is only a matter of words; "My words fly up, my thoughts remain below, words without thoughts never to heaven go."

The deceitful tongue inflicts wrongs upon other people. The distress of the Psalmist was due to lying lips and a false tongue. The deceitful tongue of Jacob deprived Esau of his birthright; false witnesses rose up against the Psalmist and filled his life with bitterness, but the greater tragedy of false witnesses was their betrayal of Jesus Christ. Deceitful tongues sent Him to the cross.

The deceitful tongue inflicts self-injury upon its possessor; it is only necessary to mention the names of Ananias and Sapphira who attempted to disguise their gift; while giving the impression that their offering was all they possessed, they stealthily kept back part of the price; in that hot moment Peter accused them of lying to the Holy Ghost, and they passed blighted out of life. A deceitful tongue is a tragic possession. Let who will be false, be you true in life and lip.

Take my tongue and make it true
Let me have no words to rue.

LOOKING UP

" I will lift up mine eyes unto the hills."

Man raises his little pyramids, God rears the mountain peaks. One of the ministries of the hills is that if we are to see them we must raise our eyes to their crests and summits. The mountains have their geographical names, but some of them have names that our experience has given to them.

Hill Difficulty was prominent on Bunyan's map: it was also familiar to the Psalmist. In his trouble he issued this order to himself, "I will lift up mine eyes unto the hills." He takes himself to task because he has been looking in the wrong direction. He had been looking down or across or away, but not up! The hills gave him the right direction for his gaze. He found, as Bunyan found, a brook at the hill-foot for his refreshment, and after that Hill Difficulty was overcome.

Hills of Desire loom before his eyes; to see them is to want to climb them. There are exiles to whom the hills of desire are hills of home, poets have sung about them, and art has set them to music. It is on a hilltop these words are inscribed:

> Here he lies where he longed to be,
> Home is the sailor, home from the sea,
> And the hunter home from the hill.

Hills of Vision are within his range of sight. Hills, too, of purpose and decision. The mountains of Bunyan's vision were called Clear; from their crests the pilgrim caught sight of the shining ramparts of the holy city. The summits of the hills offer to all of us a new wealth of vision. "I stood tiptoe upon a little hill," wrote Keats. It is the eager attitude of one who sees new things; that is what the hills of God offer to our view.

Hills of Achievement attract attention. In our generation men have stood on Everest and kindred heights, and felt themselves on the top of the world. But hills of achievement figure with solitary prominence in the life of our Lord. Quarantana witnessed His conquest of temptation; Hermon saw His transfigured splendour; Calvary's "green hill" bore the cross of His victorious passion; from Olivet His ascension prefaced His reinstatement at God's right hand. These make the hill country of the soul. Lift up your eyes, and lift up your heart·

I WAS GLAD

"The House of the Lord."

IT is the song of one who was glad to be invited to church; there may be many others who would find a cure for the ills of life and hope for their despair, if anyone would invite them to the Sanctuary. "I was glad when they said unto me, let us go into the house of the Lord."

The house of the Lord is essential to every community: the invitation makes it clear that the house was there for people to go to. That is an excellent thing; no village or township or city can be complete if there is no house of God in it. There may be houses for people to live in, employment centres supplying people with work, but all that is incomplete if the house of the Lord is not there.

The house of the Lord is accessible, distance is no final obstacle to worship; in a land where church steeples are as familiar as factory chimneys, these two things supply the two sides of life, the one for work and the other for worship, and both equally accessible and equally necessary. Worship hallows all our attachments, exalts the whole purpose of living, confesses and confirms our dependence upon God; the simple truth is that man without God is incomplete man.

The house of the Lord is attractive; some, being invited to the house of the Lord, invent difficulties, find pretexts for declining; but this man was "glad"; it was the very thing he had been waiting for. You will remember Sir Walter Scott's story of Simon Glover who, with his daughter, attended church in a season of personal trial; Simon "knelt down with the air of a man who has something burdensome on his mind; but when the service ended he seemed free from anxiety, as one who had referred himself and his troubles to the disposal of heaven."

OBJECT OF OUR FIRST DESIRE

"Our eyes wait upon the Lord our God."

CONTEMPLATION finds its true exercise, "Unto thee lift I up mine eyes, O Thou that dwellest in the heavens." Past everything else, past the summits of the hills, past sun and star the Psalmist fixes his gaze upon God. All his nature is profoundly exercised in this act of homage and desire.

> It is the soul that sees; the outward eyes
> Present the object; but the mind descries.

It is with the soul and with the mind that he contemplates the unseen and sees it!

Supplication starts from his contemplation of God; he cannot regard omnipotence and be silent; the look starts the prayer, the eye itself has language. Prayer is—

> The upward glancing of an eye
> When none but God is near.

He will hold on to God in prayer until God has mercy upon him, he has caught the spirit of importunity.

Expectation of an answer follows upon his supplication. He knows that none ever cry to God without receiving some reply; God's acknowledgments come as swiftly as the cry itself. His angels despise not any; ere the door is but half-opened they appear within, bringing the gift of God. Depressed by the contempt and scorn of his neighbours, the man casts his vexation upon God, and is sure that God will save him from the prejudices of men, and lift him up even before his scorners. The disease of inferiority has its best remedy here. All men, as all pennies, are equal, for the thing that gives them value is the superscription of the King; the rich and poor meet together, the Lord is the Maker of them all.

ESCAPED

"Our soul is escaped."

THE thing escaped is not clearly expressed but it must have been some serious peril. The three images which are employed reveal some measure of its grimness. Cruel men rose up in threatening wrath—the peril was like a wild beast ready to spring from its lair, it was like a flood of waters threatening to engulf everything, it was a net set to catch a bird, a trap for the unwary.

The Bible records a number of exciting escapes : from relentless floods, brands plucked from burning fires, a life snatched from the horns of wild oxen, a man steadied in the moment that he "almost slipped", one saved by a hair's breadth, another raised from a horrible pit, seamen rescued after all hope was taken away, even a disciple evaded his pursuers only by being dropped in a basket through a window in a city wall!

The escape effected was a completely saving experience. The soul of the man or the nation was kept from the teeth of the devourer, the floods were stayed before they could claim their prey, the bird escaped the snare. Deliverance was complete even to the breaking of the snare. The trap could not be set a second time. God breaks the power of cancelled sin and sets the prisoner free.

The power at work was not man's strategy or cleverness but God's interposition. If He had not been on the side of His people the enemy would have overwhelmed them. His deliverance confirmed the soul in its trust : this is reaffirmed in the closing sentence of the psalm. God grows upon His people by every new experience of His goodness. None perish that trust Him.

Here is James Smethan's story of his escape from a darksome mood: to him, artist and author as he was, a blessing was "a removal of the temptation to rage and scorn and indignation ; a sweetness, a satisfaction with my lot, a content with God's dealing. Take tonight, I went to chapel fretted with plenty of dark and vexing questions, all sore as to feeling ; I came away calm, sweet, fresh, all my cares gone, rejoicing in the God of my salvation."

GOD-ENCIRCLED

"As the mountains are round about Jerusalem."

THE stability of those who trust in the Lord is like Mount Zion which cannot be moved. This stability is not to be confused with obstinacy, it is steadiness not stubbornness, it is something more enlightened and sure, more refined and strong. The Apostle urged his converts not to be moved away from the hope of the gospel; concerning his own experience of persecution and trial he said, "None of these things move me"; the fears that made other men tremble had no effect on him. The Psalmist anticipated a faith surpassing the strength of hills, "We will not fear though the mountains be removed and be carried into the midst of the sea." The stability of the mountains was exceeded by the stead-fastness of human faith. Our Lord attributed to faith the power to move mountains, this is proof of the sovereignty of faith.

The serenity of God's encircled people is assured. There appear now and then souls of such radiant and resolute worth whose presence among us drives fear and uncertainty out of doors. They can be calm in a crisis; confident in purpose, resourceful in action so that other folk grow strong in their company, and timid souls find a courage above their own. They are centres of composure, patience, hope.

The security of those who trust in the Lord is His encircling presence; "as the mountains are round about Jerusalem so the Lord is round about his people". The city is set on a hill and is girdled by mountain ramparts, the soul that trusts in God is thus twice strong. Cities built on the plain required to erect walls around them for defence, and while Jerusalem had its wall it also had the encircling hills. Zechariah predicted that Jerusalem would be inhabited as a city without walls but Jehovah would be as walls of fire round about. No enemy can scale God's mountains or breach God's wall or quench God's fire. The soul that trusts in God is thrice encircled.

> In heavenly love abiding,
>   No change my heart shall fear;
> And safe is such confiding,
>   For nothing changes here;
> The storms may roar without me,
>   My heart may low be laid,
> But God is round about me,
>   And can I be dismayed?

LIKE A DREAM

" We were like them that dream."

THE first impulse of rapture throbbed within the heart of the poet when he contemplated Israel's unexpected emancipation from Babylon. The thing seemed too good to be true. You have heard people say when some glad surprise burst upon them that they did not know whether to laugh or cry, emotion reached such a pitch that either might easily happen. We are commonly conscious of unexpected misfortune but this psalm celebrates unlooked-for happiness.

The supporting intention. The first rapture of happiness did not last. The returning exiles were disillusioned, they found the home country desolate and stricken with drought, they were sorrowful and dejected, and soon found that they had to apply themselves to labour to make their own dream come true.

> They slept and dreamed that life was beauty,
> They woke and found that life was duty.

Their own labour was necessary to make permanent their change of fortune. Their prayer for flooded streams as in the southland was a prayer for the means of prosperity in a land that was hard and dry, but they had to till the ground and sow their seed to make the dream happen. That is the way with the best dreams; they rarely leap into reality of themselves; like the dreams of harvest, they come true by plough and seed-basket and hard labour; like the dreams of mountain summits, they materialise only by patient ascent, foothold by foothold, up to the topmost crest; like the dreams of the city of God, they reach reality in the earth only when men become fellow-labourers with God. Human hands must build the city, God choosing men to help Him.

BUILDING A HOUSE

"Except the Lord build the house."

THE supply of material is from God. Building houses must be one of the most interesting as it must have been one of the earliest occupations of mankind. Some shelter for the night, some refuge in rough weather, some cover from the cold was a first necessity on God's earth, and with God's material men built their houses. They went to His quarry for stone, to His forest for timber, to His pit for clay, to His mine for metal—except the Lord build the house, they labour in vain that build it.

The satisfactory design has some thought of God in it. For every true home there is a pattern in the Mount. Mortar and brick are just mortar and brick until somebody makes them something else. What we make of them depends upon the design we bring to them. God was the first architect and from His designs every true conception was borrowed. Nature is a storehouse of models and patterns, of specimens and designs.

The safety of the house is from Him. Sooner or later the house becomes part of a community or of a city and "Except the Lord keep the city, the watchman waketh but in vain". There is a city which hath foundations whose builder is God, and in that city is the Father's house of many mansions. "Go up beforehand," wrote Samuel Rutherford, "see the house you are going to and see it often." That house is built unhindered and unhelped by man, God's unchallenged and uninterrupted workmanship. In the preceding psalm God without man does not build the city; here, man without God cannot rear the house.

HOME LIFE

"Happy shalt thou be and it shall be well with thee."

HAPPY is the man that fears Jehovah; the reason for his happiness is at once given.

He shall enjoy the recompense of labour; the fruit of his toil shall be his daily bread. It often happens that one soweth and another reapeth, but here is the deeper truth that every man shall receive his own reward according to his own labour. Here as well as hereafter, "My chosen shall long enjoy the work of their hands." This is not an appeal to mercenary motives but the promise of fulfilled personality. "A wise man will desire no more than he can get justly, use soberly, distribute cheerfully, and leave contentedly."

He shall enjoy the recompense of love, domestic felicity, a peaceful, happy home. King George V spoke truly to his people when he said that the foundations of national glory are set in the homes of the people, and these foundations will only remain unshaken while the family life of our nation is strong, simple and pure. Everyone who lives in the house has a key to its felicity, for all, from the youngest to the eldest, help to make it what it is.

He shall enjoy the recompense of religion. The blessing which comes out of Zion makes the gladsome life. It has been said that religion has nothing to give to the man who is surrounded by domestic affection, but religion is the source of all true happiness; love of home and love of Zion go together. "As for me and my house we will serve the Lord"—that was the resolve of a great leader of men; it is the resolve that sets all who make it in the way of God's blessing and peace. The promise is, "Them that honour Me, I will honour."

BURNED BUT NOT CONSUMED

"They have afflicted me, yet they have not prevailed against me."

THE humiliation endured by Israel makes a sorrowful and memorable tale. The young life of the nation was spent in the bondage of Egypt and in the discipline of the desert. The language describes the nation as a slave scourged by the taskmasters: the affliction of the past comes to mind when new trials are inflicted. Remembered mercies encourage the heart to believe that in every new affliction there will be a repetition of former favour. Cruel taskmasters had laid the whip upon Israel, the nation had felt not only like a slave scourged, but also like a field ploughed. The experience had already befallen the nation, psalmists and prophets had felt it as really as if the tyrant's lash had marked their own flesh. Their love and loyalty made them feel their nation's wounds as injuries inflicted upon their own persons.

The salvation enjoyed came to them when the cords of the wicked were broken, the fetters of the masters were destroyed and the captives were set free. "Thou hast loosed my bonds." Not only was the cord of the cruel masters broken but their own prosperity was a brief and futile thing. The oppressors of Israel were like grass, incidental herbs, grown from stray seed blown by the wind or carried by the birds to the flat Eastern housetops and growing there, a poor, scanty, stunted blade which yielded no harvest. Israel survived all the troubles that befell the nation, like the bush that burned but was not consumed, or in the apostle's phrase, Israel was "cast down but not destroyed". No man can kill that which God intends to keep alive.

> One adequate support
> For the calamities of mortal life
> Exists, one only, an assured belief
> That the procession of our fate, howe'er
> Sad or disturbed, is order'd by a Being
> Of infinite benevolence and power,
> Whose everlasting purposes embrace
> All accidents, converting them to good.

FROM NIGHT TO DAY

"Out of the depths have I cried unto thee, O Lord. . . . My soul waiteth more than they that watch for the morning."

TENSION is the quality that marks this Scripture. There is intense penitence. The writer has been in depths of self-reproach but God's mercy is deeper than our depths of shame. There is intense yearning after God; more than any storm-bound seaman or night-watchman yearns for morning, this man yearns for God. At the other extreme of emotion he likens himself to a weaned child, petulant for favours missed. In some such mood Carlyle confessed: "It's a mother I want!"

The woeful cry arises from a man in the depths. There are occasions and situations when the only thing left for one to do is to cry. There are predicaments and extremities when there is no self-help upon which a man can rely; if help is to come at all it must come from some other quarter, and the only way in which it can come is in response to some summons, some bitter appeal for help. The depths in which he found himself were depths of distress; he felt that God had marked his iniquities and he recognised that if God should unrelentingly punish him he could not stand.

The welcome thought of forgiveness enters his mind and he clutches at it as the only possible hope of life. He gives himself to waiting upon God, he sets himself like a watchman set to announce the dawn, like a sentry on duty, like a man yearning for the sight of the thing he wants to see. The longer the night of storm or sorrow the more eagerly does he watch for the daybreak. The boon he craves is the forgiveness of his sin, and for that boon he will watch as men watch for the morning.

The wistful hope keeps him alert and wakeful. More than once he has stayed himself upon God in the assurance that some answer will come. God will not allow his hopes to wither as flowers wither and leave nothing but desolation behind; what encourages his hope is the assurance that with God there is plenteous redemption; when He pardons He abundantly pardons. That is the hope of the broken life. It is the passage of the soul from night to day, from ruin to repair, from brokenness to wholeness.

MAKE ME A CHILD AGAIN

" My soul is even as a weaned child."

Backward, turn backward, O Time, in your flight,
Make me a child again, just for to-night!

THERE is an attractive modesty in this little song; the man is not haughty nor his eyes proud, and he is not ambitious about things too high for him. He has not the temper of the disciples who disputed amongst themselves as to who was the greatest, who should take precedence of the rest. He has the meekness that Christ commended when He took a little child and set him before them as an example of modesty, meekness, humility, the characteristics of His Kingdom. Not all children have these qualities, but older minds can aspire to their possession.

There is an impressive sincerity about the man who writes this brief song. He felt himself a child again, accepting at first with difficulty and afterwards with contentment the early disciplines of life. He was a weaned child, had lost something for something else, and it was not easy to accept the new with the same contentment as the old. But he found himself weaned away from earthly dependence to a new trust in God; moving forward to new experiences but always sustained by the same care.

There is an encouraging tranquillity in the counsel that he gives: "Let Israel hope in the Lord from henceforth and for ever." He offers his personal experience as an encouragement to others and to his country; God's care is big enough to carry a nation as well as a man; of that this man is quietly confident, and he possesses a peace which all may share if they will. "If life is to be made interesting and worth its breath we must look on ourselves as growing children, right up to the end of our days." What is death but the weaning of our earthly childhood?

TWO COVENANTS

" David swore unto the Lord."
" The Lord hath sworn unto David."

THE Human Covenant. "David sware unto the Lord and vowed unto the mighty God of Jacob." The one thing upon which David had set his heart was the provision of a house for God; "I dwell in an house of cedar but the ark of God dwelleth in curtains." The situation seized him one day with such impulsive urgency that he resolved to take measures towards the execution of the scheme before another day had passed. There had been many bad times in his life, he had had his trials and his sins and penitences, but through it all he never allowed his distresses to frustrate his desire, he never permitted disappointment or delay to thwart his final purpose, "In my trouble I have prepared for the house of the Lord."

The Divine Covenant. "The Lord hath sworn in truth unto David, He will not turn from it." God keeps all His promises, but there are conditions attached to the promises He makes. All the conditions that God attaches to His promises are within the range of fulfilment, He does not vex us with impossible conditions. In every enterprise He plays the greater part. David was eager to find a place for Jehovah but he discovered that Jehovah Himself had chosen Zion for His dwelling. And while David was busy preparing a house for God, God was busy preparing a throne for David. "Them that honour me, I will honour." Give yourself wholly to Him and He will give Himself wholly to you.

The Mutual Covenant. The happy compromise was reached that while David was not permitted to build the House of God, he had the satisfaction of preparing such material as he could in advancing Solomon's finished scheme; for the rest God took the will for the deed. It is something to want to do something for the glory of God; even if the whole effort is beyond you, do something; like David, do something to advance the cause, make some contribution to the work, every little helps the whole. Do not despise your place or opportunity. It is the effort of every blade of grass that makes the meadow green.

TOGETHER-NESS

"How good and how pleasant is unity."

THERE is an immediate favour won by amity and goodwill; the world has long been weary of discord; suspicion and dislike have too long disturbed and distracted it. If the Christian Churches are to be peacemakers and saviours they must heal their dissensions, they must learn to do things together, to pool their resources, to get shoulder to shoulder in the campaigns of God; there are circumstances when two and two make more than four.

There is an influential fragrance about cordiality and friendliness: it is like the holy oil with which the high priest was anointed, fragrant with sweetness. Some people affect you like a bad odour, some affect you like a wholesome perfume. "He will not be able to speak to you," said a woman to Henry Drummond when asking him to visit her dying husband, "but I would like him to have a breath of you about him before he goes." There is a fragrance about the good life that will not hide. This is true of the individual life, even more true must it be of groups and fellowships; the influence of a company of good people united in spirit and in service must be the community fragrance of a cultivated garden.

There is a welcome fruitfulness suggested in the saying, "It is like the dew of Hermon." One of the spurs of Mount Hermon is called the Father of Dew. In these eastern lands of drought and heat, the dew preserves and nourishes the fruit; refreshing dews on the tired pastures, cooling dews on the sunbaked hills, encourage fruitfulness wherever they come. Christian fellowship is to have the quality that revives the fainting heart and redeems the wasted life. Some things are done in combination that could not be done by the same number of people working in isolation. The sense of fellowship contributes something to the faith and fortitude of every member.

NIGHT DUTY

"Servants by night stand in the House of the Lord."

THIS psalm is of night duty in the temple. The engaging Name is the opening theme. The Lord's name occurs in almost every sentence of the psalm, indicating how reverently and affectionately it was held by the Psalmist. It takes great devotion to write:

> O Jesus, Jesus, dearest Lord,
> Forgive me if I say
> For every love Thy sacred name
> A thousand times a day.

And we must match it with our lives. "Not every one that saith to me, Lord, Lord, shall enter into the kingdom of heaven, but he that doeth the will of my Father which is in heaven"; obedience to His will proves reverence for His name.

The service is engaging. No limit was set to the service of the sanctuary; there was constant going and coming of people, and in the evening some remained on duty for the night hours. I have visited a church where perpetual intercession is offered, those making intercession are on duty for two hours, and in relays of intercessors the work goes on night and day. John Bunyan speaks of labouring night and day to be a pilgrim; it takes a life-time to realise what is involved in so sacred a calling.

> Think not that sudden, on a minute,
> All is accomplished and the work is done;
> Though with thine earliest dawn thou should'st begin it,
> Scarce were it finished ere the set of sun.

The engaging expectation. Worship is giving to God the sacrifice of love and life; it is receiving from God the blessings of Zion. Make a habit of worship and the advantage of it will permeate the whole range of existence: in ways known and unknown, conscious and unconscious, worship gives the task of living a poise and quality that no isolated effort of our own can supply. Worship begins with living with God for an hour, and ends in God living with us for a lifetime.

A SUMMONS TO PRAISE

" Sing praises unto His Name."

You may have a singing voice ; have you a singing heart? Here is a man with a song in his heart. He sings of God's character, God's charity, God's control.

The plenitude of God in nature and among the nations is occasion for praise. The Psalmist sees God in the gathering of the mists, the flashing of the lightnings, the driving of the invisible winds. He sees the same power at work amongst the nations ; God interposes on behalf of His people so that they are preserved from the bitter assaults of their enemies. All His works were so good that His people found praise as natural as singing is to a bird.

The privileges He bestows are a further ground for gratitude. He chose Jacob for Himself and He made Israel His peculiar treasure. He chose a country for His people and He chose the people for the country. All His providences were designed to prepare His people to be the instrument of His purpose in the far future of the world. Our Lord took the same high ground with His disciples ; they had not chosen Him, He had chosen them and matched them with His hour and purpose.

The pre-eminence He claims places Him apart from the false gods of pagan peoples. The gods of the heathen are home-made. It is easy for men to make the work of their hands their idols ; they can worship money, pleasure, success, earthly glory. Anything that comes between us and God, anything that takes the pre-eminence in our life assumes the place of an idol in our affections, and an idol assumes the place of God.

'Tis the look that melted Peter,
  'Tis the face that Stephen saw,
'Tis the eye that wept with Mary
  Can alone from idols draw,—

Draw and win and fill completely
  Till the cup o'erflow the brim,
What have we to do with idols
  Who have companied with Him?

THE GREAT ALONE

"Who Alone doeth great wonders."

Yes, in the sea of life enisled,
With echoing straits between us thrown,
Dotting the shoreless watery wild
We mortal millions live alone.

THERE is an isolation peculiar to every human life. The greater
the eminence that any life enjoys the more isolated it is. But
God is the Alone. "O give thanks to him Who Alone doeth great
wonders." In creation God had no helper and in redemption He
had no adviser, He did it alone. All that was good in the experience of Israel, God did it; without Him nothing could have been
accomplished. "Art thou He that should come or look we for
another?" has the simple answer that there is no other.

There is an independence peculiar to God and derived from
Him. He alone does things; "Work out your own salvation"
has this accompanying word: "For it is God which worketh in
you." To say as Milton does that God does not need man's
labour is not all the truth. Stradivarius affirms that God cannot
do best work without best men to help Him. General Gordon
suggests the middle way, "I do nothing; I am a chisel which cuts
the wood; the Carpenter directs it. If I lose my edge He must
sharpen me. If He puts me aside and takes another, it is His
own good will. None are indispensable to Him. He will do His
work with a straw equally well."

The initiative is with God. When there was no heart to love
nor eye to pity nor hand to save, He stood beside our sinful
necessity and supplied out of His own life all that was necessary
for the saving of mankind. He remembered us in our low estate
and tore us from the grasp of our adversaries. Not to us but to
His name is the praise due, because He did it. "I have trodden
the winepress alone, and of the people, there was none with me."
He did it alone. "There is one Mediator between God and men,
the Man Christ Jesus."

Thou, O Christ, art all I want,
More than all in Thee I find.

THE SILENCED SONG

"How shall we sing in a strange land?"

THE Hebrew songs were silenced by their captivity; their oppressors added to their humiliation the desire to be entertained at their expense by the quaint melody of foreign music. Sing us the songs of Zion, they urged; but the sensitive Hebrews found it impossible to sing in their cage, the bitterness of captivity robbed their hearts of music and silenced their singing.

The songs of their native land were silenced by exile. All their happiness was centred in Jerusalem. The holy city was their chiefest joy. But in the far land of banishment their harps were on the willows. "If the Empress wishes to banish me," said Chrysostom, "let her banish me; the earth is the Lord's and the fulness thereof." This was the secret of his fortitude; but every heart that has felt deeply will understand the silenced music of the exile. There are songs that banished men and banished women cannot sing.

The songs of the exiles were silenced by harshness, "They that wasted us required of us mirth." It cannot be easy to sing because one is commanded to do it; a sob comes more easily to the lips than a song when bitter unkindness is inflicted upon the spirit. The heart of Christ surmounted the harsh conditions that encircled Him; He went with a song to His sorrow, "When they had sung an hymn they went out into the Mount of Olives."

The Christian song has been sung by exiles driven from their native land by persecution; it has been sung in dungeon and prison cell; captivity has inspired rather than silenced it; martyrs have sung it on the scaffold and at the stake. Through many a "strange land" the song persists.

THINGS TO CELEBRATE

"Great is the Glory of the Lord."

THE considerateness of God inspired this song. The Psalmist recounts God's dealings with him, and he makes his experience a key to what God wants to do for all men, for nations as well as for individuals. He celebrates God's loving-kindness, trust, responsiveness. Abandoned in the lone wilderness, the child Ishmael cried, and "God heard the voice of the lad". God is always within earshot. "We are as near to heaven by water as by land," said an early sea-rover to his men. "In the day when I cried, Thou answeredst me." Speak to Him where you are and He will answer you.

The condescension of God is gratefully recorded. "Though the lord be high, yet hath He respect unto the lowly." Kings may condescend to their people, but kings are the recipients of the condescensions of God; the kings of the earth are His subjects as well as the poor. God makes no difference between the robes of a king and the rags of a beggar; a king may have a beggarly heart, and a beggar may own a kingly mind. God's goodness enfolds both alike.

The compassion that God shows towards human weakness and frailty is the subject of continued gratification and praise. Though the Psalmist walk in the midst of trouble God will revive him, though he walk through the valley of the shadow of death, God will keep him company, though his life bear the marks of weakness and defeat, God is not finished with him yet, the processes of grace are not yet over; "Thou wilt perfect that which concerneth me" is his radiant confidence for the future. God will not put unfinished labour out of his hands. Perfection is His last word and act.

> That to perfection's sacred height
> We nearer still may rise;
> And all we think and all we do
> Be pleasing in Thine eyes.

WHAT GOD IS

"Thou hast beset me behind and before."

Is IT a comforting or a disquieting thing that God has perfect knowledge of us?

God is Omniscient; He sees and knows all things. You can keep no secret from Him. A notable author has remarked that Carlyle's eye was indeed a terrible organ—it saw everything. You know what is meant. But this, that God sees everything, that every moment "Thou, God, seest me" is either a terrible or a triumphant thought. Sin and fear make it terrible; faith and expectation make it triumphant. "Thou, God, seest me"; to be sure of that is to be sure of everything, said Margaret Ogilvy in her own dialect.

God is Omnipresent; He is everywhere; you cannot escape Him. The utmost heights open their gates to Him, the utmost depths swing wide their doors. Jacob tried flight across country but he was overtaken: Elijah fled to the mountains but God came to him; Jonah attempted escape overseas but he was caught; Judas sought the darkness but he was found out; "the darkness hideth not from Thee". Flight from Him is impossible; the true flight is to Him, that is the one escape from fear. No wings of bird nor sail of ship nor scudding cloud nor morning wind can bring you where He is not. He is inescapable.

God is Omnipotent: He is the great Power-centre of the universe. The Psalmist was not thinking of the massive works of God; he was thinking of the mystery of his own being. Behind his own making he saw God; that brought Him near; that made Him wonderful. And if sin is man's unmaking, God has the power of man's remaking. That is both man's comfort and the world's hope. There is little wonder that Ebenezer Erskine wanted this psalm open beside him when he felt that death was on its way to call him. The besetments of God never depart from us, they remain through life and through death.

A MAN'S DISTRESS

"Preserve me from the violent man."

HERE is a painful protest against the cruelties that man can practise against his fellowman. Jacob Behmen found a curious mixture of elements in the make-up of man. He can be like a wolf, cruel and merciless; like a dog, snappish, malicious, envious; like a serpent, stinging, subtle, treacherous; like a hare, timorous, frightened; like a fox, sly, thievish, artful. One of the startlingly realistic sayings of Jesus occurs in the sentence: "Go and tell that fox Herod." But the category of elements can be greatly extended. Our generation has been sadly disillusioned in the poet's estimate: "Glory to man in the highest for man is the master of things." The world has witnessed the malignity of man on a scale unparalleled in the history of the race. The ancient cry: "Preserve me from the violent man", has an impressively modern accent.

The explanation of this man's sore plight is that he has been the target of other men's enmity, the victim of man's inhumanity to man. It is strange how cruel we can be to one another; deeper than the wounds of weapons are the wounds that words inflict. This man did not find tongues in trees and sermons in stones, he found men's tongues were like serpents, their lips were poison; they set snares for his feet and prepared cords for his binding, they lay in ambush to take him.

In his plight he made supplication to God. The vehemence of his spirit and the vigour of his language are the honest outpourings of an injured heart. It would be easy to condemn the petitions he makes, but there are many hearts that feel as he did even if they have never used his words. If the wounds that inwardly bleed could find a tongue they would protest against the cruelties of men and seek the punishment or the penitence of those who do them.

The expectation he cherishes is that God will maintain the cause of the afflicted and the right of the poor. One of the helpful influences of prayer is that when we have told God our vexations, poured into His patient ear the cry of pain, new hopes arise in our despairing hearts, new lights are kindled in our night; when God comes into our thoughts, our thoughts themselves become new.

"HANDS UP!"

"The lifting up of the hands as the evening sacrifice."

LIFTED hands make supplication. "Lift up your little white hands for me," wrote John Colet to the children of St. Paul's School, London, during the Reformation conflicts. Those little white hands gave him the support of a great priesthood. It was this privilege the Psalmist desired to share, "Let the lifting up of my hands be as the evening sacrifice."

> For what are men better than sheep or goats
> That nourish a blind life within the brain,
> If, knowing God, they lift not hands of prayer?

Lifted hands confess struggle; hands have sometimes to be raised in defence of ourselves or of a cause unrighteously assailed. The gesture of the lifted hand may express protest against some excess, some evil principle, some relentless adversary. The Psalmist's struggle was with himself; he asked God to help him keep his lips from evil speaking, his heart from evil feelings, his life from evil doing. "A man touched me and I was strengthened," said Daniel. The touch of God's hand makes our hands fit for delicate tasks and responsible craftsmanship.

Lifted hands express surrender. "Hands up!" is the demand of the victorious to the vanquished. So keen is the Psalmist upon yielding his life to the will of God that he is willing to accept reproof from other men, a difficult grace. He yields his life to the custody of God, urging Him to set a watch upon his life, thus handing over to His keeping the key of all his being.

> Hold Thou my hand; so weak I am and helpless,
> I dare not take one step without Thine aid;
> Hold Thou my hand, for then, O Loving Saviour,
> No dread of ill shall make my soul afraid.

THE PRISONED SOUL

"Bring my soul out of prison."

WHAT this psalm asks from God is relief from distress, rescue from solitude, release from imprisoning conditions.

The prison was confining circumstance, irksome trouble; the dislike and distrust of men reduced the writer to despondent idleness; persecution discouraged his worship.

Many conditions may seem to prison you as within closed doors; your work is confining, your circumstances narrow, your talents are few and mean; you feel yourself a caged bird; the bars of circumstance limit your chance of a career. Your shut-in condition may begin within yourself. You may feel that you are the captive of habits you dislike but cannot subdue. Ask the Saviour to help you. He can burst the bars of your cage.

You may be shut in by infirmity. I was only a schoolboy when I listened to George Matheson, the blind poet-preacher. The wonder of that lone figure in the pulpit lingers with me through the years. Blindness had overtaken him in his student days. How far the development of his mind was disturbed by his infirmity we cannot tell. He described himself as "an obstructed life, a circumscribed life, a life which has beaten persistently against the cage of circumstance, but a life of quenchless hopefulness; barred by every gate of fortune, yet refusing to give in; overtaken by the night yet confident of the morning".

All his hymns are of the love of God; the classic is, "O Love that wilt not let me go". This was the love that liberated his spirit and kindled a light within that made the radiance of his nature master the darkness of time. Many who have suffered from the same calamity have found infinite comfort in his example of faith and fortitude.

There is an inward release that sets the soul free from depressing environments. Paul and Silas were able to sing in prison in the night; nor was their song sung under the blankets or smothered on the pillow—if they had one!—the other prisoners heard them! No confining walls could reduce them to silence. Gladness burst the bonds of their gloomy surroundings.

The story is told of a man who, through shell-shock in war, lost his speech. One Sunday evening he was at a religious service; the audience was singing in lusty volume the hundredth psalm; the impulse to sing seized him and, forgetting his weakness, he made the effort. His bonds were loosed, his speech was restored. Another life had found its way out of the prison house.

A CRY IN A CRISIS

" My spirit is overwhelmed."

COMFORT and guidance are found in the recorded experiences of men. We want to know how those who have lived before us faced the crises of their time, private and public; for what reason they failed or how they won through; by what resources they were enabled to survive and, if possible, prevail.

This man's overwhelming trouble is not related in much detail; it is good that it should be so. If the matter had been more precisely stated we should feel that the remedy discovered or the measures taken were only applicable to that particular distress or malady, whereas being generally stated we feel that our troubles are very like his, and if adversity, trial, suffering, despair, were threatening to overwhelm him and he had come to the end of his resources, we too would have felt the same.

The overcoming of trouble is the secret of the strong, especially of those who seek their strength from God. Human strength is private and not transmissible, but the strength which God gives is obtainable by all. This man made God his confidant, no other help was available, the pressure upon his spirit was great and he wanted an answer urgently; if it did not come he would go forsaken to the pit. But that was only a momentary fear; he asked power from God to amend his life, and the overwhelmed spirit was empowered to overcome.

The overrule of God is the object of his trust and his prayer: "For Thy righteousness' sake, bring my soul out of trouble." Thomas Boston suffered many vexations and delays in his approach to the Christian ministry. "Thus the Lord obliged me to have recourse to Him to do it for me. He brought me through many difficulties, tried me with various disappointments, at length carried it to the utmost point of hopelessness, seeming to be laying the gravestone upon it by my mother's death, and yet, after all He brought it to pass." Others with Boston have found that the blessings of God often come through iron gates, but they come.

A SONG'S ASCENT

"Happy is that people whose God is the Lord."

THE brevity of human life impressed the poet's soul. "Man is like to vanity. His days are as a shadow that passeth away." But we have yet to learn that the value of life is in its length. Is it not possible that we may fulfil a long time in a short time; and even if man's life is a shadow, has a shadow no value? There is a promise that a man shall be as the shadow of a great rock in a weary land; the rock in the wilderness affords a shadow from the scorching sun, and in the shadow green blades appear and flowers bloom. A great service is rendered by one who can make things a little more tolerable for someone who finds life a hard and harsh existence.

The bitterness of strife on the part of hostile men made him seek the interposition of God. He cried to be delivered "from the hands of strange children". The aliens had been cruel to him; he resented their harshness, and he recognised that only the hand of the Lord could deliver him; if the Lord would come to his aid, human hands could do him no further hurt.

> Though hosts encamp around me,
> Firm to the fight I stand;
> What terror can confound me,
> With God at my right hand?

The blessedness of recovered assurance finds immediate expression: "I will sing a new song unto the Lord. . . . Happy is that people whose God is the Lord." Blessings follow upon home and field, upon flocks and herds, yielding happiness and contentment, saving the land from invasion and making an end of strife and murmuring. Happy endings are the gift of God, but He does not keep His favours to the last. They are distributed all along the wayside in home and field and labour. The world needs more happy Christians. The new life begins that way: "O happy day that fixed my choice," and passes on to a continuous experience of the same felicity: "O Lord how happy should we be if we could cast our care on Thee." This happiness extends to the family circle: "O happy home, where Thou art loved the dearest, Thou loving Friend and Saviour of our race." And so we become distributors of the radiance of Christianity. "I am as happy as an angel," said the Countess of Huntingdon, "since I became a Christian."

UNSEARCHABLE

"Great is the Lord, His greatness is unsearchable."

A JEWISH Rabbi has given this counsel: Before you pray, repeat or read Psalm 145.

The greatness of God is unsearchable, we would not have it otherwise even if we could; greatness when it becomes familiar in a world like this ceases to be greatness. The Psalmist confessed that God had searched him but he could not search out God, for there is no searching of His understanding; He is beyond our reach. The well is deep and we have nothing to draw with. The sky is high and we have no ladder to scale its height.

The greatness of God is matched by His graciousness. That is our peace and comfort. He could use His greatness to over-whelm us as men use their power to impose themselves upon the multitude. But His power is the servant of His love, His chief greatness is His goodness.

The scope of His greatness reaches over wide fields; He is good to all, His tender mercies are over all His works; He is above partiality; He is great enough to love all mankind, great enough also to wait through long ages for the fulfilment of His purpose. The continuance of evil is not due to the weakness of God, it is due to His greatness, He is great enough to be patient and for-bearing.

The sovereignty of His greatness is clearly established: His Kingdom is everlasting and His dominion enduring. His purpose is not subject to fluctuation or revision: He is the great unchang-ing, Whose greatness is too great to be searched out by the little minds of men.

Behold, as the marsh hen secretly builds in the watery sod,
I will straightway build me a nest in the greatness of God.

"UPSIDE DOWN!"

"The way of the wicked He turneth upside down."

THE first part of the psalm celebrates the widespread mercy of God: "Happy is he that hath the God of Jacob for his help." The author enumerates the supreme qualities in God that become the advantage and the possession of those who trust in Him. God is powerful—He made heaven and earth and sea; He keeps His word with Himself and with men: He takes the side of the oppressed, the blind, the bereaved, the disadvantaged. This is the consistent witness of the psalms. It is not the speech of the imagination; it is the language of experience, and this has accepted authority among men.

The second part of the psalm announces the other side of mercy. It is with mercy and with judgment that the web of time is woven. No man can presume upon mercy. The fact of judgment is put in impressive form. "But the way of the wicked He turneth upside down." It is good for us to know explicitly where God stands, what side He takes in the often confused issues of human life and action.

The phrase the author uses is not new. The historian uses it when recording the wickedness of Manasseh and the sentence of judgment upon his reign: "Behold I am bringing such evil upon Jerusalem—I will wipe Jerusalem as a man wipeth a dish,wiping it, and turning it upside down" (2 Kings xxi. 12, 13): the prophet Isaiah uses it, "Behold, the Lord maketh the earth empty, and maketh it waste, and turneth it upside down" (Isaiah xxiv. 1): the prophet Ezekiel affirms, "I will overturn, overturn, overturn, until He come whose right it is" (Ezek, xxi. 27).

The judgments of God are as radical as the action suggests. Nothing prospers that has God against it. He can turn the malignity of evil upside down, plucking it from its place like trees uprooted by the storm. He can overturn and overturn until the evil schemes of men are as completely broken as the shattered vessel of the potter. The day of the tyrant and the oppressor is brief though the torment and anguish of it may make it seem long. The history of our time is too recent to need any illustration here, and the wayfaring man will not mistake its verdict.

The word discloses the revolutionary character of the gospel. The disciples were accused of turning the world upside down. The conflict between good and evil goes forward until the result is a world that is right-side up, and Christ is King.

SPECIALLY FAVOURED

"He hath not dealt so with any nation."

FROM the beginning Israel occupied a unique place among the nations: "You only have I known of all the families of the earth" (Amos iii. 2). The Hebrew race has been distinguished among the peoples of the world for a strong and vigorous nationalism. No other people has ever been so race-conscious. Various peoples have claimed a distinctiveness and a destiny of their own, but none with so clear a warrant as the Hebrews. "The Lord Thy God hath chosen thee to be a people, to be a special people unto Himself, above all people that are upon the face of the earth" (Deut. vii. 1–11).

We are usually more conscious of being badly treated than of being uncommonly favoured. This singer takes the generous side; he speaks of the bounties of Israel, "God hath not dealt so with any nation." He had seen this generosity in an earlier day, "He hath not dealt with us after our sins." If He were as exacting with us as we often are with one another it would go ill with most of us.

Many of the blessings enumerated are public boons; all nations share the benefit of the stars at night and the clouds that furnish rain, the grass that grows on the mountain and in the field, and the wind that vitalises the world. But the man who thinks of them and thanks God for them owns them in a special degree; to be aware of these benefits, to appropriate them with intelligence and gratitude, is to feel a sense of favour that enriches your whole existence. Appreciation makes them yours.

There are also personal benefits that come to the people who acknowledge God. They have known His healing of the broken heart, the redeeming influence of His grace, and the enlightenment of His counsel. God had put them in trust with His revelation; to be the chosen vehicle of the divine word was a privilege unshared by any other people, nor would He allow them to be unmindful that to whomsoever much is given, of him shall much be required.

A QUARTETTE OF HALLELUJAHS

"Praise ye the Lord."

"DID you ever write a song?" Thomas Carlyle asked Robert Browning, and added in a self-revealing way: "That is what I would like to do." That is what the writer here has done. A psalm without a petition is a rare thing, but this psalm is all song.

The heavenly voices are summoned to lead the anthem of creation. The language reveals an imagination greatly stirred and a soul vigorously stimulated so that he puts language into sun and moon, and bids the angels raise the chorus, leading out the praise of planet and star.

Down he swoops from heights to depths where the lower creation is summoned to take its share of song; the dragons and the deeps he names; he makes the lowing of the oxen, the bleating of the sheep, the singing of the birds, and the music of the wind all share the adoration.

> I thought all earthly creatures knelt
> From rapture of the joy I felt.

Back to human levels comes this conductor of music, summoning kings and princes and judges, the eminent of the earth, all people, age and youth and little children to take up the refrain:

> Aged men and blooming maidens,
> Young men, children sweet,
> Bring their crowns of adoration
> To His feet.

The singer calls upon his own people to mingle their praise in the universal harmonies. He directly addresses his nation, summons it to take its part; Israel is a people near to God, a special kindred of His in affinity and affection. Christ seals for us a better relationship and starts a better Hallelujah than Israel ever knew.

THE PLEASURE OF GOD

"The Lord taketh pleasure in His people."

THE invitation to write a new song (v. 1) so near the end of this volume of praise is both novel and attractive. Does it mean the attempt to keep the best wine to the last, to mount up to the very climax of outbursting song, the resolve to give the book of national devotion the highest, happiest ending? Or, does it mean that the book of sacred song is never finished? Always there will be the need of some new song; for the new experiences of succeeding generations will inevitably produce their own songs.

The praise of God is the right exercise of heart and tongue. A new song was created when God took him from the miry clay and set his feet upon a rock, but the experience of redemption is inexhaustible and so is its music. The maker of a people's songs is a great benefactor, and there are no songs that can compare with the songs of Zion. Each new age will write them new.

The pleasure of God is in His people. He might have found pleasure in other things but His mercy finds it in His people, and He knows, as all of us know in some degree, that those who give us greatest pleasure can also give us greatest pain; language cannot tell how deep were the wounds in the heart of God when the people He loved rebelled against Him.

The purpose of God gives zest to the singer; He will completely redeem His people and beautify the meek with salvation. There are bigger and better things in the years to come. No matter what comes, be glad, and live in the conviction that all things work together for good to them that love God. As your conviction is, so is your faith, and as your faith is, so will be the event, so will also be each experience. God who began a good work will continue it until the day of Christ; He is of perfect works the Finisher.

> Finish, then, Thy new creation:
> Pure and spotless let us be;
> Let us see Thy great salvation,
> Perfectly restored in Thee.

THE HALLELUJAH CHORUS

" Let everything that hath breath praise the Lord."

THE service that praise renders finds acceptable celebration in this closing song. All things were designed to glorify God; "He that offereth praise glorifieth Me", therefore praise is service. The Psalmist does not limit praise to any select place or set time. The variety of instruments suggests the range of talent employed: the horn of the priest, the trumpet of the soldier, the pipe of the shepherd, the timbrel of the woman, the harp and psaltery of the Levite are, with the capacity required for their use, all dedicated.

The subject of praise is twofold: the work of God—His mighty acts; the wonder of God—His excellent greatness. Israel witnessed the mighty acts of God in a manner unequalled by any other people. But they had never seen His mightiest act in Christ. In Him the greatness of God found its best manifestation; with Him a new speech came into being, a new language was necessary to describe the new experience, and that new language has given the world its new song.

The spread of God's praise covers all the earth. The invitation is broadcast, "Let everything that hath breath praise the Lord." This is the final call of the book to all nations, kindreds, peoples, tongues. It anticipates the song of the redeemed. "Unto Him that loved us and washed us from our sins in His own blood— unto Him be glory and dominion for ever and ever. Amen" (Rev. i. 5, 6).

> O blest communion, fellowship divine!
> We feebly struggle, they in glory shine,
> Yet all are one in Thee, for all are Thine.   Hallelujah!

> But lo! there breaks a yet more glorious day:
> The saints triumphant rise in bright array;
> The King of Glory passes on His way.   Hallelujah!

> From earth's wide bounds, from ocean's farthest coast,
> Through gates of pearl streams in the countless host,
> Singing to Father, Son, and Holy Ghost.   Hallelujah!